Perceptual Processes in Reading

Perceptual Processes in Reading

Radomir Gaspar & David Brown

HUTCHINSON EDUCATIONAL

HUTCHINSON EDUCATIONAL LTD
3 Fitzroy Square, London W1

London Melbourne Sydney Auckland
Wellington Johannesburg Cape Town
and agencies throughout the world

First published May 1973

© Radomir Gaspar and David Brown 1973

*This book has been set in Plantin type, printed in Great Britain
on smooth wove paper by William Clowes & Sons Limited, London,
Colchester and Beccles and bound by Wm. Brendon & Son Limited,
Tiptree, Essex*

ISBN 0 09 113210 X

Contents

Figures

Tables

Foreword

"Look at our spelling!"—English people sometimes exclaim—"It's so illogical and inconsistent. It bears no relation to the way words are pronounced. How on earth can we expect children or foreigners to learn that? Why shouldn't we change it?" This book sets out to answer these questions. It is—to put it simply—about what actually happens when different kinds of reader look at English words in their conventional written form, and in some possible alternative forms. To put it more technically, it is a study of the perceptual processes involved in the reading of English, and of the influence of writing systems upon the development of reading skills. This is a modest exercise in 'psycho-linguistics', written mainly for people who might perhaps still flinch from a volume with that sort of title. We try to link up several fields of study—especially 'English Language' and 'Educational Psychology'—from which convergent approaches are being made to the problems of learning to read English words written according to the usual spelling conventions.

Only a decade ago, a scholarly writer, drawing attention to the apparent modernity of seventeenth and eighteenth century statements about the English language, commented that since then "nothing new has been added to the spelling-reform controversy"; and in the terms in which that controversy had mostly been conducted, she was right. But we have written this little book in the belief that the time has now come when an interdisciplinary treatment makes it possible to transcend "the insoluble quarrel between the phonetician and the etymologist",[1] and that the centuries-old discussion about the 'advantages' and 'disadvantages' of 'traditional orthography' can be continued more meaningfully and purposefully, especially by those most concerned with the practicalities of the problem, i.e. teachers in schools, staff and students in Colleges of Education, parents of learner readers, and anyone who has to teach or learn English as a foreign language.

As far as English children and their teachers are concerned, the most important change in the reading scene since 1961 has been the progress of what has come to be known as 'the i.t.a. experiment', though in many important respects the value of the new medium is

[1] Susie I. Tucker. *English Examined*, 1961, pp. xviii and 2.

already established as more than hypothetical. The ideas put forward in this book were mostly arrived at independently of the planners of the i.t.a. programme, though they run closely parallel to theirs for some of the way, and some of the published i.t.a. material has been used. But this is not another book about i.t.a. Rather, it examines the principles that underlie the whole process of reading, including the initial teaching problem to which i.t.a. offers one possible solution, and the one most likely now to gain general acceptance. The argument of this book is of wider application, and does not presuppose any familiarity with i.t.a. material.

Some advocates of the augmented alphabet, in their zeal for promoting their cause, have tended unduly to disparage the 'traditional orthography'. The 'spelling reform' tradition is still strong, even after centuries of unavailing attack on the 'vagaries' and 'unreasonableness' of English spelling. Several reasons have been suggested (but not explored) for the persistent survival of this much-abused system of writing. What has not been sufficiently realised is that there is much more to be advanced on its behalf than the old arguments from tradition, sentiment, etymology and world-wide diffusion. Henry Bradley in fact pointed out over fifty years ago that conventional English spelling has certain positive advantages for the mature reader that counterbalance the difficulties it presents to the learner, but so far this view has not been much supported by psychological or experimental evidence.

In this book we look first at the nature of various writing systems, and then review some of the past attempts to overcome the difficulties caused by historical English spelling. The third chapter introduces some of the concepts used by more modern writers in a variety of relevant fields. The next three chapters examine the main perceptual processes—visual, auditory and relational—involved in reading, and advance the double proposition that, while a writing system based on phonemic principles is more conducive to the development of basic reading skills in a young beginner, nevertheless for a moderately advanced learner and for the adult reader a less consistent writing system stimulates the development of 'higher' reading skills and makes possible a more rapid comprehension of the encoded material. A language like Italian or Finnish, of which the spelling is consistently phonemic, presents fewer problems to the learner; but once English children have become literate to a reasonable degree they are equipped with a means of acquiring information from print at a faster rate than their contemporaries in countries where a more phonemic spelling is in general use. This is a fact of considerable importance in an age when the demand for written information is increasing in every country in the world. Chapter 7 outlines the model of the learner's attack on new words in their conventional written forms, adduces some experimental evidence, and suggests a line of approach for teachers. The final two chapters describe and discuss some further experimental work on the effects of various writing systems on the reading skills of schoolchildren and of adults.

The experimental work was planned and carried out by Dr Gaspar, and further details of it can be found in his theses for the degree of M.A. (1964) and Ph.D. (1966) of the University of London. The two authors had not then met. The book in its final form, however, is the product of collaborative discussion and re-writing. The ideas in it are our own, even if not original, and do not necessarily coincide with those of professional colleagues in the institutions where we have taught. Throughout this book, 'we' means the joint authors, or authors and reader imagined as attempting to think together; 'you' means the reader. For the sake of simplicity, we usually refer to the learner as 'he' and to the teacher as 'she', and assume that you will understand 'he or she' in each case. The word 'print' is used as a convenient general term for all written marks on paper or other material intended to be read.

Reading is a highly complex activity, though the literate adult is able to remain unaware of its full complexity while his attention is fixed on the mental products in which it results. "Good reading becomes possible", wrote C. S. Lewis, "when you need not consciously think about eyes or light or print or spelling." This book claims only to be about the background against which good reading of English becomes possible.

I

Why there is a spelling problem

The use of verbal language is a distinctively human activity. True, it is possible to describe the signalling systems used by other creatures (animals, birds, insects) as 'languages'; but only human beings can be said to use words. Of the many possible noises that can be produced by the human speech organs, some recognised combinations become charged with particular significance for each human community, and have been organised into the most complex and subtle means of communication. Speech, sounds uttered and heard, is the primary form of language. But the achievement that is uniquely human is to have devised ways of making language visible, and therefore more durable. Not only do we attach meanings to certain combinations of sounds, but we also agree that the same meanings can be attached to visible marks made on stone, wood, paper or other materials. The interpretation of these marks is what we call reading. It is easy to forget what a complicated process has been occurring while you have been looking at this paragraph. For the act of reading English words is related not only to speech sounds but also to the things or ideas which those sounds are conventionally agreed to denote. The difficulties of learning to read are always inherent in this three-way relationship of the sound, the writing system and the significance (the semantic meaning). These difficulties, however, are not the same in all languages.

Writing systems may be roughly classified into three types: ideographic, 'phonetic' and 'mixed' (that is, having some features of both of the other types). In an ideography, as the word suggests, the ideas are portrayed graphically, without any reference to the speech sounds used for the object or idea represented by each symbol. For instance, the traffic signs now conventionally adopted throughout Europe are ideographic: they convey ideas like 'turn left', 'dangerous bend', 'look out for animals', without reliance on the spoken or written words that would be used by drivers. Thousands of years ago, the Chinese invented a writing system in which every word had its own symbol derived from a simplified pictorial representation of the object to which it referred. This meant, of course, a written language with many thousands of symbols, which were (and still are) far more difficult to learn than an alphabet of a few dozen letters. On the other hand, an ideography can be understood by a great variety of people whose spoken languages may differ widely, and there is no need for it to be altered if the pronunciation of any of those languages changes.

The second type of writing system is what has usually been called 'phonetic', though the term may be misleading, as we shall explain a little later. In this type of system, the separate written symbols have no semantic value (i.e. no meaning) in themselves, but correspond only to sounds made in uttering the words in the spoken language. For this purpose, the total number of symbols required by any one language is relatively small (between twenty and forty), and is known as an 'alphabet'. Only in an alphabetic writing system can there be any question of spelling, i.e. combining written symbols in a conventional order to represent words. In some languages—Finnish and Turkish, for instance—there is an almost complete one-to-one correspondence between the written symbols and the sounds of the language; that is to say, each significant sound can be consistently represented by the same letter or combination of letters. This situation remains possible only so long as (a) the total number of significant speech-sounds used in the language is not more than can be represented by the available letters or combinations of letters in the alphabet, and (b) the pronunciation of the language does not change, or (if it does change) does so with complete consistency. For various reasons, in most languages these conditions seldom prevail for very long together. Neither of them has been true for the English language.

The writing system used for English must be classified as 'mixed', because it is at best 'historically phonetic', in that it originated in the seventh century A.D. in an attempt to represent alphabetically what were then the speech sounds of the language. Because of a series of historical factors affecting both writing and pronunciation, it no longer represents the corresponding speech-sounds with any consistency. We therefore tend to read words 'ideographically', apprehending their meaning more or less 'directly' without attempting to translate each letter into a separate sound. In this sense, English spelling can be called 'semi-ideographic'.

It should now be explained why the term 'phonetic' as applied to the writing system of any language is inaccurate. *Phonetics* is the scientific study of the actual sounds made by human beings when they speak. Now, the total number and variety of such sounds are very large—far larger than any one language makes use of. A notation that attempts to represent all of these possible sounds needs a great many symbols. Such an alphabet has in fact been devised by the International Phonetic Association, and is useful for recording the exact sounds that are heard when anyone speaks. But in the language of any community at any given stage of its development, not all of the subtle differences of sound are regarded as being equally important. Some phonetic distinctions are disregarded, while others are taken to be significant. Hearers tend to group sounds together, treating them as equivalents. A group of sounds heard and accepted as equivalents is called a *phoneme*. Each language has its own phoneme-pattern, and if it is represented in an alphabetic writing system, its spelling will be *phonemic* rather than phonetic. For instance, the first and last consonant sounds in the word *little* are different phonetically, but are both agreed to be represented by the letter *l*. The *t*-sound in *little* (as pronounced by many English speakers) is audibly different from the sound represented by the same letter in *tin*; but this difference is disregarded (even unperceived) in ordinary conversation, for it conveys no semantic distinction, although we do perceive the equally slight phonetic distinction between *tin* and *din*. On the other hand, phonetic distinctions that are semantically important to a native speaker of English may be unperceived by speakers of another language if those distinctions are not significant in the phoneme-pattern of the hearers' language. It has been related that an English missionary newly arrived in India asked to be driven at once to the Bishop—and found himself deposited proudly outside a fish-shop: the *b* and *f* sounds, phonemically distinct in English, were indistinguishable in the Indian driver's language. A phoneme, then, may be defined as the smallest unit of a spoken language which, if used instead of another, can change the meaning of a word for a native speaker of that language. This definition will, however, be examined more closely in Chapter 3.

It is convenient to note here that, with reference to the visual representation of language, we can make use of the corresponding concept of the *grapheme*. A grapheme may be simply explained as a group of symbols which are accepted as being equivalents in the representation of a unit of language. We need only to think of the variety of types that are used in printed books, or of the even greater variety of handwritings, to realise that an item of the alphabet may be represented by many differently-shaped symbols (T, t, *t*) and yet be perceived as the 'same' letter by the literate adult, i.e. the reader who has become familiar with several different sets of writing conventions. To this idea, too, we shall need to return.

We can say, then, that English spelling began by being fairly consistently phonemic; that is, that an attempt was made to represent each phoneme by one grapheme or by a consistent combination of graphemes. But to say this at once points us to the first difficulty about English spelling: that English, like most languages, has always had more phonemes than graphemes (some of which are redundant) with which to represent them. But there is a greater difficulty. Languages, like other living things, change as time passes. They are spoken by different tribes, or by foreigners; new words are added to the vocabulary; writing is done by scribes unfamiliar with the language; and so on. The eventual result has been that the discrepancy between conventional English spelling and the pronunciation to which it is supposed to correspond has now grown so great as to be a source of real difficulty to learners of the language, whether English children at school or adult foreign students. The historical background to this state of affairs need not be expounded here, but readers who are interested in it will find it briefly surveyed in Appendix A, with special reference to words that were used in the experiments described in Chapter 7. From any such survey it is obvious that the inconsistent phoneme-grapheme relationship that is so marked a feature of modern English is a problem that has many causes, and thus admits of no simple solution. Of course, not all the effects of this discrepancy are detrimental to the learner, as we shall try to show as we proceed. But there have been many past attempts to eradicate or overcome them, and some of these ideas are the subject of the following chapter.

2
Ideas from the past

(1) *Attempts at spelling reform*

The first known writer who attempted to systematise English spelling was a monk called Orm, who in about the year 1200 wrote a long work known as *Ormulum* consisting of doggerel homilies on gospel stories. The interest of the book lies in Orm's sustained and systematic effort to be consistent in his orthography. For instance, he always used a double consonant to indicate that the preceding vowel in the syllable was short, e.g. *unnder, ennglisshe*. He was the first English writer to aim at a reliable correspondence between the spoken sound and its written counterpart. But it is difficult to know whether he expected his example to be followed. Not until the spread of printed books was well under way were there any active reformers of English spelling—and by then their efforts were too late to be effectual.

The first seems to have been Sir Thomas Smith (1513–1577), who in his *De Recta et Emendata Linguae Anglicae Dialogus* (1568) suggested an alphabet of 34 letters for the English language, giving each consonant and each vowel monophthong its own symbol, and representing diphthongs by combining the symbols for the most nearly corresponding vowels. The work was written in Latin, which was then the universal medium of school education; Smith could not foresee the emergence, within the next hundred years, of a large literate population that could read only English. Of Smith's pioneer work, the historian William Camden, writing in 1605, commented rather sadly that "albeit Sound and Reason seemed to countenance" such a revised system of orthography, "yet that Tyranne (tyrant) Custome hath so confronted, that it never will be admitted". Custom has indeed offered the greatest resistance to innovation in this as in other fields.

The first man to write in English on this problem was John Hart, who assumed the name or title of 'Chester Heralt', and in 1569

5

(only a year after Smith's *Dialogus*) published *An Orthographie Conteyning the Due Order and Reason How to Write or Painte the Image of Manne's Voice, most like to the Life or Nature*. Hart sums up the arguments of those who defend the traditional spelling ("our abused Inglish writing", he calls it): they claimed that it showed the "derivation . . . of words from any strange language into ours", that it "put a difference betwixt words of one sound", and—more fundamentally—that there was no reason why any one sound could or should be represented always in the same way. Hart, however, argues (as the title of his book would suggest) with rigorous logic:

Seing then that letters ar the Images of mannes voice, ye ar forced to graunt, that the writing should have so many letters, as the pronunciation neadeth of voices and no more or less.

Despite the obvious implication that each speech-sound, however simple or complex, ought to have its own symbol, Hart's actual scheme of reform mainly consists in adding diacritical marks to vowel letters when they stand for the 'long' vowel sounds, and in using new symbols for the consonants that are represented by conventional combinations such as *th*. Thus the problem of the variety of English vowel-sounds is left only partly resolved, and the new symbols are strikingly similar to those proposed by Smith.

Another sixteenth-century spelling reformer was William Bullokar, who knew of the works of Sir Thomas Smith and 'maister Chester' (i.e. Hart) but claimed to have written independently of them. From his observation that "Experience perswadeth consent in the eye, voyce and eare", it might seem that Bullokar came near to realising that the learner might spontaneously develop analogies between written and spoken forms in spite of inconsistencies in individual symbols. But, reasonably enough, he argues the case for a "true Ortography", in which "the eye, the voyce and the eare consent most perfectly without any let, doubt or maze." The writing system that he proposed required no new letters in the alphabet, but used diacritical marks where necessary against both vowel and consonant symbols. Moderate though these suggestions may appear, their effects upon spelling reform in the Elizabethan era were negligible. All who objected to the traditional orthography encountered the tremendous resistance which tyrant custom, reinforced by the printers, exerted against any change of convention. No more successful were the attempts—such as that of Alexander Gill in his *Logonomia* (1621)—to establish a compromise between traditional and phonemic spelling. Not a single influential writer made any significant departure from accepted practice, though Gill, as High Master of St. Paul's School, may have had some slight influence on his pupil Milton's choice of spellings—for some variations of spelling were still acceptable. As regards systematic reform, Bishop John Wilkins, in his remarkable *Essay towards a Real Character and a Philosophical Language* (1668), admits that "so invincible is custom, that still we retain the same errors and incongruities in writing which our Forefathers taught us".

Other movements were beginning to operate against the innovators. From the middle of the seventeenth century onwards, the idea was canvassed that there should be some official body, corresponding to the Académie Française, which would authoritatively establish what was 'correct' English usage (including spelling). Jonathan Swift, in his 'Proposal for Correcting, Improving and Ascertaining the English Tongue' (1712), looked to an Academy not only for regulating the English language, but also for 'fixing' it beyond the possibility of further change. His contemporaries, Addison and Pope, devised unfulfilled projects for dictionaries based on the usage of the most 'correct' writers. Meanwhile several dictionaries had already been published; the earlier ones aimed only to explain 'hard words' in the English language, but later works attempted to include the whole range of words in general use. The general effect of all these activities was to reinforce prevailing practices (which were largely determined by the customs of the printing houses), and thus perpetuate accepted spellings.

In 1755 was published the most famous of English dictionaries, that of Samuel Johnson, who himself compared it to those compiled by the academies of France and Italy. In his preface, Johnson dismisses Swift's 'Proposal' as a "petty treatise", and he confesses, in the light of his own seven years' labour on the Dictionary, that the expectation (which he too had once entertained) "that it should fix our language and put a stop to those alterations which time and chance have hitherto been suffered to make in it without opposition" was one "which neither reason nor experience can justify". A lexicographer will be only an object of derision if he "shall imagine that his dictionary can embalm his language". Yet Johnson, while recognising that the vocabulary of a living language must change, accepts as his first task that of "adjusting the orthography, which has been to this time unsettled and fortuitous". He distinguishes between two kinds of "irregularities" in spelling: on the one hand, those

7

that he regards as "inherent in our tongue"—i.e. long-established anomalies that are so much part of the language as to be unalterable— and, on the other hand, those that are the product of mere accident or ignorance. Established spellings, however anomalous, Johnson accepted. Only where variant spellings of any word were current did he think it "proper to enquire the true orthography". In such cases, he tried to settle the matter by reference, not to the pronunciation, but to the language from which the word had been derived: as, for instance, choosing the spelling *entire* rather than *intire* because the word had passed to us from the French. But "even in words of which the derivation is apparent", he writes, "I have often been obliged to sacrifice uniformity to custom"; and therefore "in compliance with a numberless majority", he had to write both *convey* and *inveigh, deceit* and *receipt, fancy* and *phantom*.

Johnson's great Dictionary, then—both through its own intrinsic merits of comprehensiveness and scholarship, and also because of the literary reputation of its author—tended still further to dis- courage any radical reform of English spelling. Indeed its noble and humane Preface is perhaps the most thoughtful statement ever made about the inherent difficulties that beset any single-handed student of language, be he innovator or merely recorder. In his 'Plan' of the Dictionary (1747), Johnson had written of the hopeless absurdity of trying to establish a spelling which reflected a con- tinually changing pronunciation, and also of the less absurd but still (as he thought) impracticable idea of a spelling based on one-to-one correspondence of sound and symbol.

Such would be the orthography of a new language, to be formed by a synod of grammarians upon principles of science. But who can hope to prevail upon nations to change their practice, and make all their old books useless? or what advantage would a new orthography procure equivalent to the confusion and perplexity of such an alteration?

Johnson could not foresee the development and application of a com- plete phonetic notation on scientific principles, nor could he imagine a 'new orthography' being of any practical advantage whatsoever.

Even in Johnson's lifetime, several scholars were seeking a different way round the problem, as will be shown in the next section. Others, however, continued in their attempts to remove what they still considered to be the root of the trouble—the traditional system of spelling. In America, the proclamation of political inde- pendence seemed to provide a good opportunity for shaking off other forms of 'tyranny', and Noah Webster prepared an impressive list of changes for the spelling of words in his Dictionary. By the time the work went to print in 1806, however, only insignificant alterations had survived, and the vast majority of American spelling remained virtually the same as that used in Britain at the end of the eighteenth century.

In the middle of the nineteenth century there was launched a fresh (and ultimately more successful) campaign against Conventional English Spelling (which we shall hereafter refer to as CES[1]). It began in 1848 when Sir Isaac Pitman, the inventor of a new short-hand system on a phonetic basis, and A. J. Ellis, philologist, mathematician, musician, and founder of modern phonetics, proposed a new alphabet of forty letters. By 1870 Ellis had abandoned hope of any success for an alphabet including new letters, but believed that there was a better chance for his later invention, 'Inglish Glossic', which used combinations of ordinary letters in such a way that each speech-sound would be consistently represented. This system, though following the same lines as those of Elizabethan reformers, avoided the necessity of diacritical marks, and was more scientifically related to English phoneme-patterns. This new movement towards spelling reform, coming at a period of educational expansion, gained many adherents; a speaker at the Social Science Congress in Birmingham in 1868 described CES as a 'heterography' and warned of its restrictive effect on the general spread of education. Interest in such ideas was now sufficiently widespread to lead to the formation of a Simplified Spelling Society, whose members were especially active at the beginning of the present century. Yet in their pamphlets attacking CES, there is still the same almost despairing tone as was adopted by their Elizabethan predecessors: Walter Rippman speaks scathingly of men having 'a certain fondness for the existing orthography because of its very irrationality, of its constant unfitness to fulfil its professed aim in representing

---

[1] We choose this abbreviation in deliberate preference to TO (Traditional Orthography), which has already been given some currency by Sir James Pitman and others. What we consider important about English spelling is not its traditional nature, nor its assumed 'correctness', but rather the fact that (like all other writing systems) it is a particular form of conventional behaviour and must be understood as such. CES means the spelling *now* conventional: at earlier stages, before spelling became conventionally fixed, one can only speak of the accepted orthography of the period.

pronunciation'; W. W. Skeat re-asserts the priority of spoken over written language; William Archer complains that the stock argument against reform 'inverts the order of reason by placing the eye, in matters of language, before the ear'. Still English spelling remained unchanged. Nor has much come of any twentieth century proposals for radical and universal reform, which range from Bernard Shaw's scheme (backed by the royalties of his best-selling play *Pygmalion*) for a new forty-letter alphabet, to the more scholarly proposals (in 1959) of Dr Axel Wijk of Stockholm, who enumerates eighty-two principles of a 'Regularized Inglish'.

All this discussion of the desirability of a revised spelling, however, has not proved fruitless. In 1949 a group of reformers, including Mr I. J. (now Sir James) Pitman and Mr M. Follick, succeeded in introducing in the House of Commons a Private Member's Bill which (had it become law) would have enforced a revised spelling. During the debate on the second reading, all the old arguments and counter-arguments were repeated; the measure was then rejected by a narrow majority. This and subsequent events indicate the weakening resistance to any change in CES. The promoters of the Bill changed the direction of their activity, and in 1953 Mr Follick introduced a more limited 'Simplified Spelling Bill' which called for an investigation into the use of such a spelling for the purposes of teaching to read and of providing for a transition to CES. This measure was accepted. It required that fifteen years from the date of its acceptance a report should be submitted on the degree of success achieved by the use of a simplified spelling. In October 1961 began the enquiry, under the guidance of the University of London Institute of Education, into the use of a system called 'Augmented Roman' as an initial teaching alphabet, now widely known as 'i.t.a.', and several reports on the progress of the experiment are now available.

'The history of English Spelling Reform', according to the *Encyclopedia Americana* (1957), 'is one of great enthusiasm and effort but of tragically small achievement.' Such a judgement is now questionable. Centuries of enthusiasm and effort have at last resulted in the adoption, for an admittedly limited purpose, of a writing system more logical and more consistent than the accepted English spelling has ever been. This achievement is not small, nor is its lateness tragic. Its significance can be better appreciated if we next survey some of the previous principles on which English-speaking children have been taught to read.

(2) *Methods and rules*

Of course people have learnt to read English despite all the difficulties posed by its spelling conventions. At least since the Elizabethan period, scholars and teachers, however critical they have been of the *means* at their disposal (i.e. the accepted orthography) have addressed themselves also to the *methods* by which the reading of English might most effectually be taught. "Methods for learning to read", wrote John Dewey in 1898, "come and go across the educational arena, like the march of supernumeraries across the stage. Each is heralded as the final solution to the problem of learning to read, but each in turn gives way to some later discovery." But this succession of past ideas is not entirely without sequence or pattern, and a selective review of some older approaches may serve to indicate perennial problems that teachers still have to solve.

As was shown in Chapter 1, a spelling problem is inherent in the use of an alphabetic notation, and a crucial difficulty in English has always been the adoption of the Roman alphabet without any augmentation, that is, without adjusting the number of written symbols to that of the phonemes of the language. Thus in effect an 'alphabetic' method of teaching to read was inherited along with the set of 23 or more letters.[1] The first stage of learning to read consisted of learning the so-called 'names' of the letters. In the next stage these 'names' were applied to the reading of syllables and words. But in English the letter-names did not always convey the speech sounds for which those letters were supposed to stand (e.g. *h, q, w, y*); some letters (e.g. *c, g,* and all the vowel-letters) were ambiguous; and discrepancies were most evident in some of the commonest words.

One of the first known scholars to raise his voice against the 'alphabetic' method was John Hart. In 1570, only a year after his *Orthographie*, he published his other major work, *A Methode of Comfortable Beginning for All Unlearned Whereby They May be Taught to Read English, in a Very Short Time, with Pleasure; so Profitable as Strange.* The scope and essence of Hart's method are indicated in the following extract:

We have been heretofore taught to misname our letters, to the hindrance of all the willing to learne . . . Now you may teach your scholler, to

---

[1] In earlier stages of English writing, the symbols *i* and *j* were interchangeable, and were *u* and *v*, and sometimes *c* and *k*.

remember the letters by the names of the portraytures, first the five vowels . . . You may not name the l, m, n, nor r, as you have been taught, calling them el, em, en, er: but give them the same soundes, you do find in their portraytures, without sounding of any vowel before them . . . M-oul, N-idl, R-ing.

The 'portraytures' in the book are pictures of objects; for each letter there is a picture of something for which the usual word begins with that particular letter. The first speech-sound uttered in the usual pronunciation of that word should be used, according to Hart's method, as the name of that letter. But the procedure, not altogether strange to us even now, could not be as successful as Hart expected. This letter-naming is not really suitable to the English language: even in initial positions, as well as elsewhere, some letters were bound to stand for more than one speech sound. To this day we are left with the discrepancy between the 'name' by which we denote a symbol used in the conventional alphabet (ay, bee, cee . . .) and the sound or sounds to which that symbol may correspond.

A few early thinkers began to approach the problem along different lines. Given that there was an ineradicable discrepancy between the written and spoken forms of English words, there still remained a fundamental question about the relative efficacy of the visual and auditory modes of perception as vehicles for ideas.

Why should it be thought impossible that the eye (though with some disadvantage) might as well apply such complications [i.e. complex systems] of letters or other characters, to represent the various conceptions of the mind; as the ear, a like complication of sounds?

The question was asked in 1661 by John Wallis, mathematician, grammarian, student of medicine and a founder member of the Royal Society. The above passage, from a letter to his friend Robert Boyle, formulates one of the basic questions of the present study: how far is it possible to 'recognise' print by visual perception alone, entirely separated from auditory elements? That such recognition is possible was demonstrated by Wallis in 1662 when he satisfied a meeting of the Royal Society that he had trained a deaf and partly dumb boy to recognise English words in print. Unfortunately the records of the experiment do not sufficiently indicate the methods, circumstances, duration or intensity of the training that had enabled the boy to make so many complicated bonds. We do not know, for instance, whether Wallis had brought into play any other physical sense such as touch, as happened when the deaf and blind Helen Keller learnt the mastery of language over two centuries later. Thus the case of Wallis's deaf boy does not in itself provide us with any means of assessing the real disadvantages, especially in terms of time and effort, of having to learn the skill of reading without help from the spoken forms of words. It is still questionable whether the amount of time that has to be spent on teaching a totally deaf child to read might be better devoted to equipping him with some alternative mode of communication.

Yet Wallis's enquiry has a twofold significance. In the first place, he realised that normally speech sounds, in the conventional combinations of a particular language, are the primary symbols of concepts, while the letters of the corresponding alphabet, being used to represent speech sounds, are the secondary symbols. It is rather surprising that Wallis does not take into account the discrepancy factor noticed by earlier writers, but simply asserts that 'letters are, with us, the immediate character [i.e. notation] of sounds, as those [are] of conceptions'. But in the second place, Wallis is a pioneer of educational pyschology in further postulating that, under some conditions, written symbols might become the primary rather than the secondary symbols. "There is nothing in the nature of the thing itself", he wrote, "why letters and characters might not as properly be applied to represent immediately, as by intervention of sounds, what our conceptions are." Wallis supported his contention by an argument which is not (or at least, not directly) relevant to English spelling. He pointed out that the Chinese language makes use of special characters (ideographs) which do represent 'things and notions' independently of the spoken forms of words, and again that throughout the Western world numerals and arithmetical and scientific symbols are always written in the same way, whatever the language, and are understood "without attending to the sound of words". The implied question which he left for later generations was whether it might be possible or even advantageous to think of reading English words in a similar way, i.e. quasi-ideographically. This line of thought remained undeveloped for over two hundred years.

A diametrically opposite approach was adopted in the eighteenth century by Thomas Sheridan (father of the dramatist R. B. Sheridan), who, after a brief career as an actor, devoted himself to teaching and lecturing on elocution. In a discourse delivered at Cambridge in 1759 he went so far as to assert that, at least in an alphabetic system,

Written characters have in themselves no sort of virtue, nor the least influence upon the minds of men, and the utmost extent of their artificial power can reach no further than that of exciting ideas of sounds.

(We may note here that over a century later the 'ideas of sounds' were given a specific name when J. B. de Courtenay in 1895 used the word 'phonemes' to denote the psychological counterparts of speech sounds.) In Sheridan's main work, *A Course of Lectures in Elocution* (1762), he showed that he was aware of the distinction between the two chief systems of writing: ideographic, "which had ideas for its immediate object, without reference to sound", and alphabetic, "which had sounds for its immediate object, and whose chief end was to give an exact representation of them, as in musical art." Ideography he saw as merely a primitive and experimental stage leading to the invention of letters "which by being made symbols of articulate sounds, became capable of conveying knowledge in as extensive a manner as speech and with equal ease and celerity." In this last claim Sheridan has the support of most modern experts, who maintain that silent reading is possible at a remarkably *higher* speed than speech, though the degree of difference may be limited by such factors as the training and background of the readers, and the level of difficulty of the material. Sheridan also pointed out the advantages of an alphabetic system for teaching people to read, and for the easy setting of printing type. Evidently he also had in mind an ideal alphabetic system which should be as accurate as musical notation, ignoring the fact that a mere alphabet cannot encode such features of speech as pitch, tone, pace and so on. It must be remembered that the technical means of recording speech sounds remained virtually unchanged from the time of the invention of the alphabet until the end of the nineteenth century. Sheridan was particularly scornful of any system "which professed to have sounds for its object, but was little solicitous about accuracy in making them." The traditional English orthography, he thought, did not take advantage of either of the two chief systems, while retaining almost all of their disadvantages: it was dependent upon the spoken language and yet was very difficult to learn. Sheridan in fact realised that the Roman alphabet "by no means squared with our tongue", and afforded fewer characters than were required to represent the speech sounds of the English language. He found himself in difficulties in preparing the figures for both the phonemes and the graphemes used in English. Like other reformers, he really wanted a simplified system of spelling, not least for the reason that "in Britain particularly, [the art of reading] is almost universal, since even the children of peasants are instructed in it." But unlike other reformers, he realised that in practice the obstacles to a complete reconstruction of spelling on strictly phonemic principles had remained insuperable, especially since the introduction of printing. Instead, he proposed (and set about compiling) a dictionary on phonemic principles:

. . . a dictionary in which the true pronunciation, of all words of our tongue, shall be pointed out by visual and accurate marks . . . the whole to conclude with a key to the pronunciation of the English tongue, whereby the learner may know how to pronounce most words in our language at sight, notwithstanding the irregularity of our spelling.

Perhaps Sheridan hoped that such a publication, by familiarising learners and teachers with phonemic writing, could lessen the resistance to a more comprehensive spelling reform. But the really important element in his work is that he realised, however dimly, that any phonemic notation for common use presupposes a measure of agreement about what speech-sounds are in fact used for each word, i.e. a more or less standardised pronunciation. No dictionary, as Johnson knew, can embalm a living language; nor can any phonemic spelling system remain phonemic unless it continues to correspond with a generally accepted pronunciation, of which a dictionary can be compiled. Sheridan's somewhat unscientific advocacy of 'elocution' thus points forward to the pioneer work of Ellis and Sweet on phonetics and pronunciation, to Daniel Jones's devising of a general phonetic alphabet, and to his great *English Pronouncing Dictionary* (1923). But it also raises the questions of how far a standard pronunciation of a language so widely diffused as English is either possible or desirable, and therefore of the limits within which a phonemic alphabet, even for a restricted purpose such as initial teaching, can be useful.

A third, but less profitable, approach to the problem of learning an inconsistent orthography was that adopted by Robert Nares, who in his *Elements of Orthoepy* (1784) offered "a distinct view of the whole analogy of the English language", in which he described general tendencies observable in the relationships between written and spoken forms of words. Those words which did not conform to such generalisations were classed as exceptions, and Nares invited his readers to discover more such general tendencies which would reduce the number of exceptions. Nares's use of the word 'analogy' must not be understood to suggest that he was a predecessor of modern psycholinguists such as Mowrer who relate analogy to the concept of mental images. Really Nares was working towards the notion of 'rules' in the relationship between written and spoken forms of English words; indeed, the second edition of his work, without any change of content, was entitled "General Rules for the Pronunciation of the English language." This concept, which appears to offer some alleviation of the difficulties of learning English spelling, has subsequently been adopted by some eminent linguists, and notably by Sir William Craigie in his *Pronunciation of English* (1917) and *English Spelling, Its Rules and Reasons* (1927). But such 'rules' have proved to be unhelpful guides, even for adults, to the problem of *learning* to read English. A. J. Ellis roundly asserted, in his *Spelling Difficulties* (1870), that "any rules that can be given are so full of exceptions that they are practically worthless". Despite the fact that there are many cases in which a moderately advanced learner can tell quite accurately from the spelling how to pronounce a given word, it is also true that there are no rules which would enable him to pronounce any word with complete confidence that he was right. Even Axel Wijk, author of *Regularized Inglish* (see p. 10) has to admit that there are many English words for whose pronunciation on the basis of spelling "the rules that could be laid down would often be rather complicated, and they would only cover a certain proportion of the words in question". Significantly, 'rules' of this type have never been taught to any great extent as an aid to learning English, not even when 'rules of grammar' formed an important part of the school curriculum. The rules, it seems, are of the type that can only be perceived by those who have already learnt to read the words to which the rules apply. This approach, unlike those that we have previously examined, seems to come to a dead end. Yet even so, something can be gained from Nares's analytical method. If it is possible for an experienced reader to deduce that some words in English are 'regular' and some are 'irregular', then the teacher should be able not only to build up the learner's confidence in those areas where the rules are most nearly reliable, but also to predict the areas where 'irregularity' will be an obstacle, and to observe what kind of analogy the learner himself discovers. We shall return to this point in Chapter 7.

Broadly speaking, until the end of the nineteenth century there remained two unreconciled accounts of the perceptual processes involved in reading: one holding with Wallis that it was possible to use letter-groups as primary symbols, i.e. not requiring the intervention of sound, and the other following Sheridan's doctrine that the chief objective of an alphabetical system of writing should be an accurate representation of the spoken language, i.e. that the visual percepts of letters cannot directly elicit any response in terms of semantic meaning, and that the mediators must be what are now called phonemes. The question took a new form when Gestalt Psychology opened fresh vistas to educators. As early as 1885 Cattell showed its application to some phenomena involved in reading, when he proved that written words are perceived faster than the same number of letters in isolation. The 'whole-word' or 'look-and-say' method of teaching came into fashion, though it is interesting to note that it had been propounded long before the 'Gestalt' theory. Comenius had put forward its basic idea in the middle of the seventeenth century by suggesting that pictures could help beginners to read whole words; this, he believed, would eliminate the boredom of learning to read by spelling out separate letters, and the method was applicable to any language. Comenius was active in England for only a brief period before the Civil War cut short his work here, and the 'whole-word' method had no further support for more than two centuries.

The supporters of 'phonics' did not yield their ground. They pointed out that the 'look-and-say' method left the child entirely dependent on the teacher's assistance, and that no use was being made of the advantages offered by an alphabetic system of writing. By the middle of the present century a compromise was reached. In Great Britain most teachers started with the 'whole-word' approach and later gave some 'phonics'. The discussion continues, mainly localised on two points, the time of starting phonics, and the appropriate amount of practice in each method. F. J. Schonell, in his *The Psychology and Teaching of Reading* (1946) lays emphasis on the 'whole-word' approach. On the other hand, Hunter Diack, in *Reading and the Psychology of Perception* (1960), argues the need for a higher proportion of 'phonics', and points out some misconceptions in the 'look-and-say' method, which are in his view the product of a wrong application of the Gestalt Psychology. Clearly the two positions are not irreconcilable. A recent investigator, Pearson, found that "in general, the knowledge of sound-letter association is of great practical importance for the development of reading ability, for the promotion of quick and accurate visual perception of the whole word; that children, irrespective of whether they are taught by a phonic or by a visual method, who gain proficiency in reading, are proficient both in the knowledge of letter-sound associations, and in the quick and accurate perceptions of the whole words". Such findings suggest that before much progress can be made with any *methods* of teaching to read, "the importance of a knowledge of letter-sound relationships should be clearly recognised". The problem of how this knowledge is developed still calls for thorough investigation, and this involves, among other things, a reconsideration of the *means* by which sounds are represented in writing. Does this seem merely to take us back to the same problem that exercised the sixteenth-century reformers? Yes, in a way—but with two great advantages available to us: a greater knowledge of the physiology and the psychology of perception, and the means of analysing more closely the nature of the obstacles presented by the existing writing system. The key word now is *investigation*.

(3) *Modern investigation*

Literacy is not a simple aptitude; it is a complex system of skills which some children acquire more readily than others. And since slowness in acquiring these skills may be due to any one, or more than one, of a number of causes, treatment must depend upon diagnosis, and will vary according to which causes are revealed.

(M. M. LEWIS: *The Importance of Illiteracy*, 1953)

It is characteristic of modern writers on any problem connected with reading to stress two related points: the complex nature of the process itself, and consequently the variety of ways in which it must be tackled. This attitude is a natural consequence of the development of psychology as a field of study, the scientific exploration of the workings of the human mind both in itself and in its relations to other minds and to external phenomena.

In the first half of the present century, the centre of attention tended to shift from the nature of the language to the nature of the learner; more recently it has focussed again upon the relationships between the two, in the developing study of psycho-linguistics. It is impossible here to review the whole realm of psychology in relation to the learning process, and we assume that the elements of that knowledge are either known or available to most readers of this book. We select only a few lines of modern enquiry that are relevant to our specific topic and also typical in their scope and method, and we reserve some for further treatment in the following chapter.

One of the most eminent of modern psychologists, Sir Cyril Burt, in a *Psychological Study of Typography* (1959) sets out a problem connected with reading in terms that could not have been used in previous generations:

If we take the 'phoneme' as the unit of information, the English language presents us with a fairly well-defined ensemble of alternative elements— 12 vowels and 37 consonants—which the printer proceeds to encode by using an alphabet of 26 visual signals.

He proceeds by pointing out that "there is always some degree of visuo-mental interference or 'blur' which impedes the accurate transmission of visual information", and his study is one of many that have been devoted to the kinds of 'blur' that readers may experience. Burt shows how some of the variable factors in print have an effect upon reading, and more particularly upon the rate of comprehension. His work is mainly concerned with the influences of the size and shape of individual letters of the alphabet, and investigates the effect of such variables upon advanced readers looking for information in scientific journals. This closely specialised study of one aspect of reading is relevant to the topic of the present book, in which we are concerned with other variables and their effects upon the development of reading skills. Burt's work does not stand in isolation, but is one of a group of related studies in the same field, for it is typical of the modern investigator that he sees his own work as part of a continuing process which is both collaborative and dialectical. One researcher (E. C. Poulton, 1959) has shown that the style of type is a significant factor in efficiency of reading. M. A. Tinker and others established in 1956 that differences in the alignment of letters also have an influence, and that the horizontal arrangement of lines is the most conducive to speed; this is explained in terms of the perceptual processes associated with different eye-movements (see Chapter 4). At about the same time, Nahinski found that a 'square span' arrangement of print, in which the phrases are arranged in small double-line blocks, would permit a more economical use of the vertical dimension of the visual span. Again Lukiesh and Moss have pointed out the important effect of 'leading' (i.e. space left between adjacent lines of print) upon readibility. We mention all these studies in one single small part of the field because our book too is concerned with the influence of the arrangement of printed signs upon efficiency of reading. In particular we discuss the effect of sequences of letters *within words*—i.e. spelling: the kind of arrangement that results from the system of writing that we have called CES—and the effect of that arrangement both upon the development of reading skills in the average child and upon the efficiency of the advanced reader. This point will be developed in the next chapter.

Before resuming it, however, we want to draw attention to two important differences between the earlier students of 'the reading problem' and their modern successors. First, the use of the word 'investigation' in the heading of the present section of this chapter is intended to indicate that the main emphasis now is upon 'experimentation' rather than 'discourse'. Because reading is now recognised to be a highly complex activity, any approach to the problems we have outlined so far must be cautious and tentative. As Sir Cyril Burt has pointed out, while more research into the question of reading methods is still needed, one must be prepared to see one's own cherished ideas either disproved by immediate experiment or exploded later on. Too many factors are involved in the problems of reading to permit any firm conclusions, especially in a single study. There has even been disagreement, for instance, on whether or not difficulties in learning to read are in fact attributable to the inconsistency of English spelling. On experimental evidence W. R. Lee concluded that its effects were negligible, though most others, notably Downing and Gardner, have found grounds for believing the opposite. A further reason why hard-and-fast conclusions are not yet possible with investigations of this sort is that, in general, it is acknowledged that experimental circumstances may significantly differ from circumstances of normal work. This difference is likely to be more pronounced in a complex field of learning such as reading, where so many factors interact and fluctuate from stage to stage. It is no longer possible to speak of 'the problem of reading' or to expect one simple answer. A child's success in learning to read may be influenced by social, economic or personal factors such as the amenities of his home, the income of his parents, their example in reading to themselves or to him, the emotional security or deprivation of the child, his motivations for learning, and so on; it will also be related to his physical and intellectual endowments, to his rate of maturing, to the competence of his teachers, and to both the methods and the means by which he is taught. It is the latter group of factors that we are here investigating.

This leads us to the second important difference between earlier and later writers on reading problems. The existence of a variety of hypotheses and approaches is now taken for granted, and indeed encouraged. "It is quite possible, even advantageous, to have more than one theory in the same area; for example, psychoanalytic, learning and self-theories, so long as each brings order into some part of the area, and each stimulates further observations" (P. E. Vernon, 1964). What we propound in the remainder of this book is no more than one possible line of approach, based indeed upon theory, and supported by some relevant experimentation, but essentially calling for further investigation and perhaps development. We examine the correlation between, on the one hand, the development of elementary reading skills and also of the 'higher' skills needed by an 'advanced' reader, and on the other hand the use of certain means (i.e. writing systems) for this purpose. We have already made a distinction between *means* and *methods*; we are primarily concerned with the former, but of course no given means can be evaluated without reference to the method of its use, and the choice of any writing system as means must have some implications for the method by which its use can best be mastered. Each successive stage of investigation stimulates new theoretical formulations.

But even more important is to bear in mind that judgements about means must be related to *ends*. Our survey of ideas from the past will have shown that, although there may always be inherent and perhaps insuperable difficulties about the direct introduction of a phonemic language for all purposes, yet for some specific purposes, such as teaching the rudiments of the reading process, it is possible to devise more efficient means than CES, if we make careful use of the findings of modern investigators about the nature of that process itself. It is in this area that psychology, physiology and linguistics now have common ground.

3
Some more modern concepts and terms

In the course of this chapter, we make a double approach to the problems of learning to read English, along lines suggested by modern developments in psychology and linguistics. One kind of approach might be described as 'atomistic' and the other as 'structuralist'. By 'atomistic' we mean 'concerned with identifying and describing the smallest possible units of an organism or activity'—in this case, mainly the phonemes and graphemes to which we have already referred. By 'structuralist' we mean 'looking first at an organism or activity as a whole, in order to discern its nature by means of the patterns or structures made by its constituent parts'. Both kinds of approach are relevant and necessary in trying to understand the activity of reading, in any language or writing system. Literacy is related on the one hand to spoken language, which both children and adults experience as a 'flow' of sound within which they gradually discern patterns of repetition and contrast; but on the other hand it is related to sequences of visible marks which will not 'flow' in the same way until their details have been identified. Reading thus involves both 'smallest units' and 'patterns'; atomistic and structuralist theories are helpful in different ways with reference to different stages of attainment.

We can start by saying something—briefly and in very general terms—about the science of linguistics, which has emerged as an autonomous field of study only during the last half-century. Linguistics is concerned with the scientific study of language: on the one hand, with the study of particular languages, not as means to any further end, but simply as phenomena to be described and analysed as completely and accurately as possible, like other objects of scientific investigation; and on the other hand, with the study of language in general, and with the formulation, if possible, of principles of linguistic description and analysis. Its attitude towards its subject-material is objective. All languages and all forms of language equally merit attention. The 'standard' or 'accepted' or 'literary' forms of a language are no more important to the linguist than are its social or regional dialects. Since speech is the primary form of language (and many languages have still not been written down), his first concern is with the speech-habits of a community. On this basis, the description of any language will comprise three inter-related parts: *semantics*, which describes the meaning of words and sentences; *syntax*, which describes the ways in which words are combined within sentences; and *phonology*, which describes the ways in which sounds are combined to form words. Or, to put it another way, there are said to be two 'levels' at which any language can be analysed: the 'primary' or *syntactical* level, dealing with sentences as combinations of meaningful units (such as words or morphemes), and the 'secondary' or *phonological* level, dealing with sentences as combinations of sound-units or phonemes which are in themselves meaningless. It must be noted here that these 'levels' of analysis are used to refer to what the linguistic analyst does, not what the speaker does. They do not necessarily correspond with 'levels' of mental activity on the speaker's part.

Let us apply this to the relatively simple basic human means of communication, speaking and listening, before we come back to the more sophisticated activities of writing and reading. A message occurs (to use a neutral word for the moment) in a speaker's mind; it is then structured into a sequence of words capable of analysis at the syntactical level, and issues as a sequence of sounds capable of analysis at the phonological level. This, as far as we can tell, is the actual temporal order of events. The listener has (as we all know) the slightly more difficult task, for the order of events is reversed for him. He receives a sequence of sounds; then, having received a sufficient number of them, he perceives a syntactical pattern, and only when that pattern is complete can he arrive at the semantic apprehension of the message which initiated the process in the speaker. Unlike the speaker, he cannot foresee the next stage of the utterance, though the time-interval before he perceives it is usually brief. He has to store auditory information in his memory for a second or two before it is used in the formation of a syntactical pattern.

With writing and reading, however, a further completely different set of physical activities are called into play, in addition to those required in speaking and listening, before the semantic meaning is communicated. The writer has to make visible marks on a surface;

the reader has to move his eyes in order to perceive such marks and associate them with meanings. Let us leave aside for the moment the question of what happens when a writer is putting a message on to paper. But it is clear that the reader has to perform a whole series of operations before he can associate what he sees with language in any form or with semantic meaning. For a child, these operations are less easy and less 'natural' than those associated with speech and hearing; they take longer, and therefore in the early stages of learning there must be a longer time-interval between the perception of the parts and the apprehension of any semantic whole. This is why the consideration of 'minimal units' is more relevant to the very earliest stages of reading than to the more advanced stages.

We can sum up what we have been saying about reading by representing the process diagramatically, using the concept of 'levels', not quite as the linguistic analysts do, but rather with reference to the perceptual processes of a reader, and indicating the appropriate minimal units at each level (Figure 1).

Figure 1: Diagram of perceptual processes

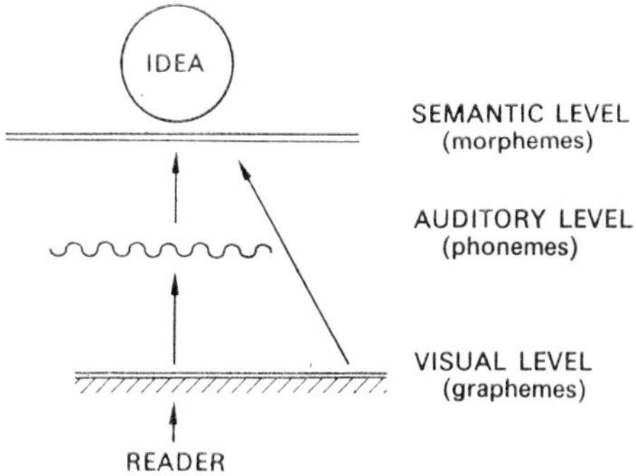

Broadly speaking, the above account holds good for any language and for any writing system, though you will remember that an ideographic system implies a more direct relationship between the visual and the semantic levels (as is indicated by the continuous arrow in the diagram), and we have for the time being disregarded the fact that advanced readers of alphabetic languages also may appear to by-pass the auditory level. The possible forms of relationship between the visual, auditory and semantic levels are crucial to our enquiry. We shall also consider how the 'idea', which we have provisionally represented as a circle, may take different patterns, with different effects upon the reader. The diagram will be developed at later points in the chapter.

The immediate point is that learning to read, by whatever method, is inherently difficult, however pleasurable; for efficiency in reading requires a complex set of skills. Moreover, each of these skills is itself a complex matter. "We begin to use the term *skill* only when many receptor and effector functions are interlinked and related within an order of significant succession which possesses an inherent characteristic of direction and moves towards an issue regarded as its natural terminus" (Sir Frederic Bartlett). We can classify the skills required for literacy according to the major perceptual phenomena and processes that they involve—visual, auditory and relational— and they will be discussed more fully in Chapters 4-6. The development of these skills is now an important objective of educators all over the world. But how best to promote that development is a question to which many different answers can be given, for the choice of means and methods must vary according to the readers, and according to the language—and especially according to the kind of writing system involved. Let us briefly develop these points with reference to English.

The discussion of how best to promote reading skills has sometimes tended to become confused because of differing emphases being laid upon the needs of several distinct categories of reader. We try to distinguish, from this point onwards, between the needs of the average child on the one hand and the interests of the educated adult on the other. Within this latter category, one could make a further distinction between the adult reader of his own native tongue and the student learning English as a foreign language. It is reasonable to assume that different levels of progress call for different procedures; that at any one stage, the development of one skill may require the use of some means that are not conducive to the development of some other skill; and therefore that no single means or method, in isolation, is to be considered as superior to others. Conventional orthography and various types of special script, 'phonic' and 'look-and-say' methods of instruction, may all be useful if employed at the right stage.

In particular we are here concerned with the influence of writing systems upon the development of reading skills. Now the system that is used in CES has certain well-acknowledged advantages for the educated native adult reader. It is an instrument of great subtlety; it preserves the etymology of words; it distinguishes between words that sound alike; it is independent of localised forms of pronunciation. It may also (as Henry Bradley pointed out in 1919) be conducive to the development of certain 'higher' perceptual processes. But it does not necessarily follow that CES is the most suitable system for a beginner. It cannot be an exact representation of speech, and its 'irregular' letter combinations make it difficult for beginners to recognise the written counterparts of spoken words that they know. It is not entirely suitable for learning even such a basic reading skill as proceeding from left to right along a horizontal printed line.

If then we are to reconcile the needs of the learner with these of the educated adult, we must take into account the differences in the perceptual processes that occur at different ages and different levels of literacy. For a child who is at the early stages of learning to read (whatever the system of writing used) is dependent upon vocalisation, or upon some form of 'inner speech', to a far greater degree than an adult, who may be able to proceed 'directly' from visual percepts to the semantic meaning of words. Let us compare two widely separated stages of this development.

Sounds are among the most important experiences of early childhood, and the attaching of significance to speech-sounds is the essential basis of language. A baby soon learns that, of the many vocal sounds that he can make, some are more likely than others to produce a response from his mother or some other adult. Out of the spontaneous rhythms of his earliest babble, the child selects, by imitation and by experience, the sound patterns that have meaning for other people. Specific combinations of speech-sounds become charged with emotional experience, or become associated with objects and events in his world. Speech is meaningful to him long before he meets the written word. The establishing of auditory patterns is essential to the growth of both his experience and his vocabulary, and long into his school days he will need a rich nourishment of spoken language. By the time a child is 'ready' to learn to read, his spoken vocabulary is already remarkable, and it is probable that he can perceive (i.e. recognise) an even larger number of spoken words than he can use. But on the other hand, at this stage each written letter of the alphabet seems to represent for him a difficult complex pattern. The physical act of perceiving it is as much as he can manage. Even one or two years later, an average child is unlikely to be able to perceive more than two or three letters without moving his eyes. There are physiological reasons why a young child can speak and perceive speech at a remarkably higher rate than he can read. By contrast, an educated adult recognises on the average more than one whole word during each eye-fixation of about 0·2 seconds; that is an ordinary line of print in about one or two seconds. Thus he can attain a substantially higher rate of comprehension in silent than in oral reading, or than in listening to speech. It has been reckoned that English is usually spoken at about 150 words per minute, while an average person in England or the U.S.A. can read at 250 words per minute or faster. The full implication of this contrast between the two stages of physical and perceptual development will be brought out in subsequent chapters. First we must introduce some other concepts and terms that are used in this book.

Whether a reader be predominantly 'visual' or 'audile' or of any other type with regard to the perception of print, what he has to do, if he is to take any advantage of his spoken vocabulary in learning to read, is to 'translate' written signs into the corresponding sounds. In an alphabetic system—that is, a code in which (at least in principle) the symbols stand for single sounds or phonemes—this 'translation' has to proceed, in its elementary stages, from individual letters or small letter-groups. Whatever the ability of the learner, the process of reading has to start with the perception of the shapes of certain print units. We have already mentioned the difference between children and adults in the number of eye-movements that they have to make in reading. There is a further essential difference: even though the physical area covered in one eye-fixation may be the same in two readers, the kind of print-units that can be 'simultaneously perceived' will differ according to the development of certain related skills. What is called the *visual field*, therefore, is the amount of visual information that is actually 'sensed' by the reader in a given period of time and can be used, directly or indirectly, for the derivation of semantic meaning. During one eye-fixation, the visual field may amount to no more than a single letter, or it may be a digraph, a syllable or morpheme (i.e. the smallest meaningful unit of language, such as prefix or suffix), a special group of letters (see Chapter 6), a word, or even a group of words.

The corresponding percept (i.e. the mental result of perceiving the usable visual information obtained in one eye-fixation) is known as the *span of recognition*. This percept is especially significant, not only because the width of the span of recognition is considered by some experts to be the best measure of a reader's 'maturity', but also because it seems to have a determining effect upon the next step in the reading process, the interpretation of the unit of print perceived. If a reader is able to perceive a whole word simultaneously or as a unit, he may be able to derive the semantic meaning directly, without a significant intervention of auditory elements. But if he is still at the stage of a narrower span of recognition—when during one eye-fixation he cannot perceive more than an individual letter or a sequence smaller than a morpheme—he seems to have to translate the visual percepts into some auditory counterparts before he can proceed. As we often need to remind ourselves, the letters of an alphabet stand not for concepts but for sounds; it appears to be very difficult to manipulate visual percepts that correspond to 'meaningless' units of print without any help from speech sounds or their traces.

The width of the span of recognition (and consequently the type of print-units that can be simultaneously perceived) must play a very important part in the *rate of comprehension,* or the efficiency of reading proper, the process by which word-groups form thought-units, which in turn are combined to give meaning or comprehension. Now, it must be remembered that some research workers have strongly suggested that there may be a significant discrepancy between this kind of efficiency in reading and the 'rate of thinking' in general. In other words, what is usually referred to as 'intelligence' cannot be the only factor affecting this crucial 'span of recognition'. It is therefore reasonable to assume that, besides 'intelligence', besides the method and the amount of instruction, a significant factor in the development of reading ability is 'readability' of the material. The ease of visual reception, in so far as it depends upon such technicalities as the size, style and boldness of letters, the arrangement of lines, 'leading' and so on, may have a bearing upon the span of recognition, and has been discussed in a number of studies (see pp. 19–20). Little attention, however, has yet been given to the question of how the development of the span of recognition might be affected by the use of different systems of writing.

There is some evidence, however, that the degree of consistency in what has been called 'grapheme–phoneme correspondence' has a varying influence upon this development at different stages of reading ability. A degree or type of correspondence that enhances the span of recognition for a moderately advanced reader may create a barrier to the perception of print for a beginner. Throughout this book we are maintaining, on the one hand, that in an alphabetic system of writing no meaningful recognition of print is possible before the reader is able consciously or unconsciously to interpret letters in terms of phonemes, and that a system of writing that observes phonemic principles, and therefore is most conducive to such interpretation, favours the development of the span of recognition in the early stages of learning to read. Such a system would be of benefit to all normal children (that is, those without any remarkable physical or mental defect) and especially to the average child who is otherwise 'ready to read' but finds it difficult to over-come the inconsistency in sound-values of the letters as used in CES. Moreover, a phonemic script could also be useful, although in a different way, to the foreign student who wishes to make use of his reading to learn to speak the language correctly in respect of its speech-sounds. "I do not think it an egzajeraeshon", wrote Gilbert Murray in 1926, "when surten forreners sae to me, az dhae ofen duu, 'We kan read Inglish, but we duu not atempt to speek it, bekauz dhat is liek lurning anudher langgwej." On the other hand, we are equally maintaining that, at a level of reading ability where the meaning can be derived almost directly from the configuration of written words, the span of recognition may in fact be widened by the use of a writing system such as CES which discourages the making of hard-and-fast connections between individual graphemes and phonemes. The old assumption that spelling reform necessarily implies the universal adoption of a phonemic spelling, or some near approach to it, must be challenged. No one system of writing should be considered as 'best' for all purposes and for all levels of reading ability. In order to establish these two points, we must discuss more fully the concepts of 'grapheme' and 'phoneme', and some related ideas.

A learner can be considered to have mastered the essentials of any phonemic system of writing when he is able to respond to each of the written signs by overtly making the corresponding sound. If the learner knows the meaning of the spoken words so produced, these sounds may be said to serve as 'vehicles' from the written signs to the writer's ideas. At a more advanced stage, however, the reader is able to understand the message without any 'overt' utterances, i.e. merely by 'looking' at the printed signs, even if he is encountering some of the words in their written form for the first time. In this case, what sort of 'vehicles' take the reader from the printed signs to the writer's ideas ? The question is more complicated than it may appear. In an alphabetic system of writing, the con-figuration of any word as a whole is largely a coincidental product of the shapes of the written signs associated with certain speech-sounds; it does not in itself provide any clue to meaning. If—to take an imaginary example—we were to encounter the word *ditter*, we could get no help as to its meaning from knowing words that look like it, such as *bitter* or *dither*. We might perhaps be able to deduce from its context whether it was a noun or an adjective or a verb. But what we could do at once with reasonable certainty is to pronounce it. In a completely phonemic language such as Finnish, Turkish or Serbian, it is possible to pronounce any word at sight. And in any alphabetic language, it seems that the learner first has to translate individual signs into some elements of inner speech; they have been described as 'partial responses' (Osgood), or 'auditory sensations' (Vernon) evoked by the visual perception of letters.

The smallest significant elements of this 'inner speech' are what, in the rest of this book, we refer to as 'phonemes'. Thus the term *phoneme* will be used to designate a specific cerebral activity rather than some physical event in speech. This definition falls within the wider concept of the 'phoneme' as originally formulated by de Courtenay (see Chapter 5). It is true that the term has already been used by many modern scholars to denote some elements of 'overt' speech; some of them find it difficult to explain phonemes as psychological phenomena, and prefer to use the term for certain 'families' of speech-sounds. But it seems even more difficult to think of the phoneme as a physical event in overt speech. For although practically all significant manifestations of speech can be accurately detected, recorded and analysed by modern machines, the 'boundaries' between one phoneme and another can only be determined by subjective criteria. It is impossible to decide which speech-sounds belong to the same 'family' (i.e. which variations in physical sound do or do not semantically change words of a language) without observing the behaviour of native users of the language. Change of semantic meaning is of course a question of psychological responses rather than of objectively definable linguistic classifications. The *phoneme*, therefore, we take to be *the psychological counterpart of the smallest significant unit of spoken language.*

Correspondingly, we use the term 'grapheme' for the psychological counterpart of the smallest significant unit of written language. In an alphabetical system of writing each grapheme corresponds either to a relatively uniform visual representation of a letter of the alphabet or (more often) to a 'family' of such representations regarded as equivalents. A letter of the alphabet can be printed not only in various sizes, styles, colours and degrees of boldness, but in different shapes (capitals or minuscules, italic or roman, and so on). The actual sense-data received may vary considerably without changing the essential significance of the letter in its phonemic value or its semantic implications. For instance, the experienced reader will have learnt to recognise the word DANGER as being 'the same' word as *danger*, even though each of the six letters is represented by a differently shaped visual signal in the two sequences. Visual perception in reading has to develop so as to enable the reader to abstract from the print only the essential information, ignoring for most purposes the non-graphemic features. The learner reader of English has somehow to learn that the slight visual difference between DANGER and DANCER is graphemic, whereas the more obvious difference between DANCER and *dancer* is not.

It is important to remember that at different levels of literacy there are significant differences in the phoneme–grapheme interaction. Even if we could suppose that a child could learn to perceive the letters of an alphabet in terms of graphemes (i.e. to recognise them as being 'the same' in spite of their obvious variations of shape), he certainly could not convert these percepts into meaningful units unless he had already associated them with some auditory percepts of speech-sounds. He will perceive the difference between DANGER and DANCER only if he already knows the sounds of the spoken words. At this stage, a knowledge of phonemic sequences seems to be essential to the very perception of graphemes. But an adult with abundant practice in reading seems to have become able to short-circuit the process, as it were, by avoiding the perception of words in terms of phonemes, or at least by reducing to a minimum the intensity of auditory sensations in silent reading.

The complexity and variability of grapheme–phoneme interactions may be further illustrated if we think about the other side of this communication channel. What is happening when somebody is writing? If he is writing from dictation, and using an alphabetic system of notation, he must first perceive certain chains of phonemes and then translate them as best as he can into a corresponding sequence of graphemes. What is happening, then, when an experienced writer is expressing his own thought in such a system of notation? He may perhaps be able to do so without any conscious interposition, i.e. without perceiving any significant units of 'inner speech'; but most of us do in fact make 'slips of the pen' such as suggest that we have been 'talking to ourselves' while writing. It is difficult to imagine how a beginner could dispense with these elements of auditory mediation even in 'silent' reading or writing.

The overt activity of making marks on paper we may think of as being governed by the graphemes in the psychological sense described above. The grapheme has the role of a visual *image*. "The behaviour is the response to an image", as K. E. Boulding says, "not a response to a stimulus, and without the concept of an image the behaviour cannot possibly be understood." An 'image', in the sense in which we here use the term, may be defined as "a mental representation of something not by direct perception of it, but by memory or imagination" (O.E.D. s.v. *image*, 5), or, more relevantly to our present problem, as "an experience which reproduces or copies in part and with some degree of sensory realism a previous perceptual experience in the absence of the original sensory stimulation" (Warren, *A Dictionary of Psychological Terms*). It is now widely taken for granted that such images are built up on the basis of experience. In this respect the concept may be reconciled with behaviourist theories; but it seems to imply that the human mind has certain inherent characteristics that cannot be included within the simple 'stimulus-response' formula. No one knows what 'laws', if any, may be valid for images; perhaps one can only say, as Miller and Dollard wrote in 1945, that "it seems probable that they follow the same laws of learning as do other responses, even though the responses producing these cues may possibly occur within the organising centres of the brain". But we may also note the importance attached to 'conditioning' by many psychologists who are far from being strict behaviourists. It is certainly open to question whether every act of learning can be called 'conditioning', though it might still be granted that conditioning, when it does occur, is a kind of process of learning. We shall show that the 'conditioned-image' approach to the problem of grapheme–phoneme interaction in reading is of limited value, and raises problems that are not explicable in behaviourist terms.

The earliest experiments to have any direct bearing upon our enquiry were those described by Clarence Leuba in 1940. His main objective had been to find out whether sensations (e.g. of light and sound) could be conditioned to objective stimuli in the same way as the overt responses, i.e. by an "automatic, mechanical and unconscious" process. The results consistently obtained in the course of ten years of experimenting led him to conclude that the two categories of responses, the subjective and the objective, are equally conditionable, and Leuba suggested that all mental images might in fact be 'conditioned organic sensations'. The objection that all of Leuba's subjects, while being trained, were under hypnosis was answered when D. G. Ellson obtained similar results with subjects in their normal state of mind.

Now, up to a point, the elements of training in Leuba's experiments are the same as in learning to read, in that they involved the pairing of visual and auditory percepts. But the crucial difference is that the percepts in reading are far more complex: instead of noting a simple flicker of light, the learner must perceive the shapes of different letters; instead of noting a single tone, he must differentiate about forty phonemes; instead of making a one-to-one relationship, the reader of most languages may have to associate the same letter with different phonemes. This vast difference in complexity is only partly compensated for by the circumstance that the pairing of different percepts continues for longer in learning to read than in the experiments of Leuba and Ellson. On the basis merely of such experiments we would have to assume that learning to read even a consistently phonemic notation is achieved through the creating of multiple associative bonds between letters and sounds, and we might explain the nature of these bonds by saying that the presentation of a letter evokes the corresponding phoneme. But this in itself would be a large and bold assumption, and it would not satisfactorily explain the ability of a learner to read new words, i.e. combinations of letters that he had not met before.

Certainly, when it comes to learning to read a notation such as CES, the 'conditioning' explanation becomes very difficult to accept. What images then occur to the learner when he meets an unfamiliar and irregular word in print? And why? No previous experiments supply any answer to those questions. Even if such conditioning as was used by Leuba might produce associative bonds between single graphemes and corresponding phonemes, it does not take us very far with CES, where any unfamiliar word may mean a new and possibly unique combination of graphemes. In order to proceed, we must go back briefly to theory, and consider the idea of 'patterning' of images. You will notice that we have now reached a point at which atomistic accounts of linguistic and perceptual activities are inadequate.

It has been maintained that images may become organised at a higher level than that of the smallest significant units. Certain sequences of phonemes can form patterns of auditory units; certain sequences of letters can form patterns of visual units. Under certain conditions, it may be supposed, associative bonds can be formed between these larger units of the two sense modalities. Such bonds would help to explain the 'chain-reaction' in reading progress which is noticeable in a learner of English when he reaches a moderately advanced stage. Even when the eager young reader is presented with a totally unfamiliar word, he will react in terms of sequences of speech-sounds rather than trying to respond overtly to individual letters, whatever the method by which he has been taught. The formation and development of the bonds responsible for such reactions cannot so far be demonstrated by direct experimental evidence; but there are nevertheless sound theoretical reasons for believing them to exist.

In spite of a great variety of formulation, fundamentally similar views about 'patterning' can be found in many studies. One writer maintains that, in one sense, the process of learning is "a spontaneous activity towards perceptual organisation", and speaks of "indivisible patterns of sounds" which could be treated as 'Gestalten,' but in the sense of gradually structurised units rather than something innate. Such patterns of sounds had been discussed by both Sapir (1925) and Hull (1943). The patterning of responses in general was treated by Dollard and Miller (1950). Another researcher rejects the idea of memory as merely a passive registration of events and holds that "it gives evidence of being constructive activity of the organism and one which results from the arousal of dynamic processes". It has been pointed out that even what we call 'simple' perceptions are in fact complex additive ones, with a "purposeful character". This interpretation of perception is implicit in the work of Bartlett, who uses the concept of 'schema' (singular) or 'schemata' (plural), maintaining that "all incoming impulses of a certain kind, or mode, go together to build up an active organised setting" in which mental images have a governing role. All this testifies to the belief that the human mind, in all its functionings at every level, does not merely receive information; it selects, it re-arranges, it associates, it organises into new wholes.

This patterning is sometimes explained in terms of operations which are performed by the brain. For instance, Grey Walter refers to a 'scanning mechanism' which is constantly searching for patterns. Certainly modern physiology seems to be able to give some account of the phenomena which for convenience we have called 'patterning of mental images'. This at least gives us some ways of conceptualising possible solutions of psychological problems: by thinking for instance of an 'assembly cell' as solving the jig-saw puzzle created by the scattered stimuli, or again as 'firing' the single cells, either simultaneously or in a temporally ordered sequence. But the physiological approach to patterning can not altogether explain the purposeful character of perception. It is necessary to take into account some psychological factors, and especially the one often referred to as *drive*. "The effect of drive is to organise longer sequences of unit acts into instinctive, habitual or insightful patterns of responses" (Madsen). That patterning is of this dynamic character is now taken for granted by some students of Communication Theory. We shall return later to the importance of 'drive' in learning to read. We may note here that many writers, even those who cannot accept the term 'mental image', do use terms that are closely associated with such concepts as 'schema', 'structure', 'patterning', or 'assembly cell'. For convenience we use the term 'patterning of mental images'; it provides a way of describing the relationships between pronunciation and spelling, and of interpreting the formation, functioning and consequences of the bonds that the reader makes, and the 'mechanism' that he builds up. Patterns of this sort are not accurately describable in words, but for the moment at least we might think of each mental operation in reading as being a portion of a chain.

Let us return briefly to the question that we left at p. 32: when somebody is writing, how are the graphemes formed in his mind? What might be the previous links in the chain, and what kind of links are they? Clearly, the answers must depend on the writing system that is being used. In a true ideography, such as an educated Chinese might use, the graphemes (the visual images that control the writing movements) will be 'released' either by the semantic meaning of the whole word, or (less probably) by the phonemic sequence that represents the corresponding spoken word. In a purely phonemic system, the graphemes will usually be elicited each by the corresponding phoneme. But in a mixed system such as CES, the processes cannot be formulated so easily as in the other two cases (see Figure 2.) Some few words will be written phonemically; but for others, it has been found that there are two principal varieties of stimuli that elicit the 'correct' graphemes, not singly but in groups or strings: (a) auditory perception of the whole word, especially if the conventional spelling is so irregular and distinctive that no analogy is likely to be made with any other word; and (b) certain phonemic chains, smaller than words, but not necessarily corresponding to spoken syllables. The responses to both these stimuli may be further complicated by the effect of analogy with other familiar words. The possibilities of error (i.e. failure to produce the graphemes required for a conventional spelling) seem to be manifold—as any teacher knows from experience. Yet it is equally well-known that millions of people do learn successfully to read and write in such a system. Though the patterns of mental images required for using CES are complex ones, and are not structured in any readily discernible way, they are evidently not as completely chaotic as we might suppose if we looked only at the variety of the grapheme–phoneme relationships; nor is the human mind incapable of dealing with such complexities—otherwise, of course, you would not be reading this book.

Figure 2: Diagram of perceptual processes in CES

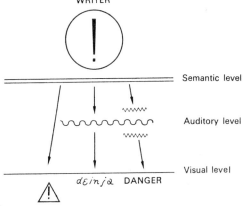

We can conclude this chapter by pointing to some possible parallels between problems of reading a complicated writing system, and those of mastering the grammar of one's own language. One of the most important recent developments in psycho-linguistics is the work of Noam Chomsky and the whole climate of thought that he has largely created in the last decade. His writings, being primarily concerned with linguistics in the sense described at p. 23, deal mainly with spoken language and with its analysis at the syntactical level; they are not easy to read without some prior knowledge of this field, but they are based upon important concepts which can be related in several ways to the questions we are considering. Chomsky has been the most influential critic of the purely descriptive and behaviouristic approach to language. The grammar of a language, he has maintained, is not something mechanical that can be constructed solely on the basis of a corpus of written texts, or even of a sample of spoken utterances; rather, it is something 'generative' that operates to 'produce' syntactical structures when people are talking. Grammar, like all language, is creative in character; its nature is such as to enable people not merely to imitate sentences that they have heard, but also to produce sentences that have never been uttered before. For Chomsky, truths about language correspond with truths about the human mind and about human nature. In this essential respect he is making a larger statement of the idea that we put forward a little earlier, that the perception and creation of patterns or structure is an essential characteristic of the human mind, and that the ability to read quite unfamiliar words is a phenomenon that cannot be accounted for in strictly behaviourist terms.

In respect of syntax, Chomsky has drawn a distinction between the 'surface' structure and the 'deep' structure of a sentence. We need not go into his whole theory of transformational grammar, but this one important idea within it can perhaps be brought out by means of a simple illustration (not from Chomsky). Take the sentence: *The farmer gives his horses food every day.* This is a straightforward way of expressing in English the mental apprehension of a situation in which there are five essential and inter-related elements: a man, some animals, a material substance, an action involving all three, and a recurrent time element. In English, the words denoting these elements are usually arranged in an order like that of the sentence quoted. If the same mental apprehension of the situation were to be expressed in French or German or Latin, the corresponding words would more naturally occur in a different order. Even in English, essentially the same mental image might be conveyed in different ways, according to which of the five elements we chose to indicate first: *The horses are given their food by the farmer every day,* or *Food is given to the horses every day by the farmer,* or even *Every day sees the farmer giving the horses their food.* Each of these sentences has a different 'surface' structure, which generates the particular grammatical forms in each case, yet each is related to an underlying 'deep' structure. The hearer of the sentence in any of its forms apprehends the situation in its totality by his own re-ordering of the elements presented to him via the surface structure. The parallel that can be drawn with the topic of this book is that English words are often apprehended in their totality only after some comparable re-arrangement of a conventional order of letters, which in turn have been perceived within a structure. One might almost hazard the notion of a 'deep' spelling underlying the several possible spellings that are produced by different writing systems. Certainly, a 'sense' of structure as an essential feature of the human organism is a central concept in the most influential modern school of psycho-linguistics.

Again, Chomsky, using words with his own distinctive meanings, distinguishes between *performance* and *competence* at the syntactical level. By *performance* in a language he means the whole body of utterances actually produced by speakers of that language; but from this can be eliminated a certain number of utterances (perhaps made under abnormal physiological or psychological conditions) which a native speaker or hearer would normally rule out as 'ungrammatical', or not typically part of his language. (How do you react to the 'sentence', *The horses every day food the farmer gives* ?) A grammatical sentence, in this sense, is simply a sentence acceptable to the native speaker, and his awareness of what is grammatical is what Chomsky calls his *competence*. This competence, which enables him to generate new sentences, is perhaps partly intuitive, and also is based on his total previous experience of the language. Correspondingly, we suggest, skill in reading written words, whether familiar or unfamiliar, may be related to a similar kind of linguistic competence, partly innate or intuitive, partly based on early experience of relationships between visual percepts and certain features of spoken language. The study of the reading process requires on the one hand an analysis of the writing system concerned, and on the other hand the characterisation and specification of the resources which the reader brings to a text. These resources include not only his given physiological and psychological equipment but also the product of all of his previous linguistic experience, including supraphonemic features such as stress and pitch, which are not represented by any marks on the page.

If you now turn back to the simple figure of the reading process (Figure I), you will see that it needs to be modified in several respects. What we called there the 'idea' is always more complex than a neat isolated circle. Whether it is a sentence or only a single word, it has some kind of structure in itself and usually some relation to larger structures. It might be stylised as $\wedge$. It can be represented in a standardised way because at this level it is independent of the writing system to be used, and is not essentially influenced or determined by any 'surface' structures. But at other levels, as we noted on p. 37, the idea may generate widely different visual forms, each of which has to be read by a different combination of perceptual processes. So we might modify the figure as in Figure 3.

There is one important corollary of this. The more experienced the reader, the more rapidly does he reach the semantic level in

Figure 3: Modified diagram of perceptual processes

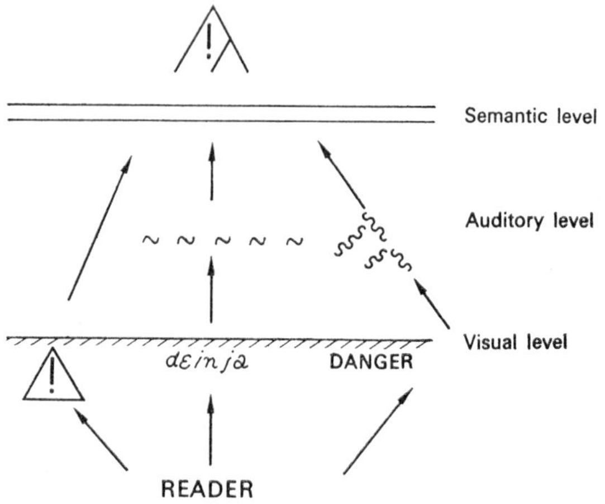

his reading, and the more important in that process is the structure both of the thought and of the words by which it is mediated. The mature reader perceives words in their relations to other words, and may perceive single letters only in their relations to each other within the word. The beginner is less able to perceive structures in reading. A child is, of course, normally accustomed to perceiving speech in this structural way: he hears and understands complete words and even sentences without breaking them down into their constituent parts. But when he starts learning to read an alphabetic system he has to proceed from much smaller units, if only because of the physiological limitations of his visual mechanism. He cannot at first see whole words as well as the details of letters. Therefore progress at the lower levels of reading and writing depends much more upon the nature of the writing system than it does upon the nature of the thought. The educator's approach therefore may need to be more atomistic at the elementary stages, and become more structural as the bonds between spoken and written language develop.

4
Reading by sight

The activity of reading is the exercise of a complex of skills functioning together to give a degree of comprehension that satisfies the
reader. Provided that we remember that these skills are inter-related,
we can now examine them in turn, beginning with the group related
to sight. The immediate goal of the purely visual activity in reading
might be described simply as the perception of printed signs in
terms of graphemes. But we have already noted that the process by
which this stage of perception takes place is not the same in children
as it is in educated adults. At a high level of reading ability the
reader recognises words as wholes, and an inconsistent grapheme–
phoneme relationship has no adverse effect upon the rate of comprehension. At the early stages of learning to read, when the average
child needs more than one eye-fixation to perceive a meaningful
string of graphemes, any complication in the relationship between
single graphemes and phonemes may hamper the proper formation
of the 'visual field'. In this chapter we explain this point further,
and go on to show how a writing-system which makes it necessary
for an average child to perform two or more eye-movements before
he can with any reasonable degree of certainty translate his visual
percepts from print into the corresponding auditory percepts of
speech is liable to produce difficulties at the 'short-term storage'
level; these in turn will produce a number of regressive eye-
movements, which may become habitual. We must note, however,
that a writing-system that has an adverse effect upon the initial
formation of the visual field may have a different effect upon its
subsequent growth; this point will be developed in Chapter 6.

The pioneer of the research into visual activity in reading was
Emile Javal, whose *Physiologie de la Lecture et de l'Écriture* was
published in 1906, and who became a fervent advocate of spelling
reform in France. His scientific study of eye-movements led him to
realise the advantages of a consistent and economical writing system,

on both psychological and physiological grounds, and he was convinced that actual French orthography was contrary to common sense, particularly when applied for the purpose of initial teaching. He was able to support this view by devising ways of recording the oculomotor behaviour of adults in decoding printed passages, though (probably because of certain imperfections in the devices then available for recording eye-movements) Javal and his co-workers gave no corresponding data for young beginners in reading. Although he refers to one of his assistants, M. Lamare, as the first to adopt this approach to the overt symptoms of silent reading, it is Javal who is now considered the real originator of a research project which led to one of the essential discoveries in this field: that the eyes of a reader do not glide, as it is sometimes assumed, along the lines of print, but perform a series of jerky or 'saccadic' movements.

Since Javal's time, oculomotor behaviour has been of increasing symptomatic value in the study of problems bearing upon reading. Upon these overt symptoms have been based important studies of visual perception, as well as assessments of methods for teaching reading, and even studies of 'thought units'. On the basis of such work it is now possible to describe more fully certain changes in oculomotor behaviour that seem to accompany the development of some reading skills. Beyond this, however, we must proceed with caution. "Eye-movements are in no sense causes of good or poor reading; rather they are symptoms of the manner in which one reads" (G. T. Buswell). It was at one time mistakenly assumed that reading efficiency could be improved by working directly on the eye-movements. Reading skills are more complicated than that. We must relate oculomotor behaviour to the whole process by which phenomena are apprehended by the mind, to differences in that process at various levels of reading ability, and to the role of these differences in some 'higher' perceptual activities such as dynamic patterning. Even so, all this is the process, not the goal, of reading. So, in comparing the oculomotor behaviour of a child and an adult reader, we must remember that these observable symptoms can be no more than a starting point, for there may also be differences in the ways in which visual data are processed at various levels of literacy, in the power of psychological 'drive', and in the degree of comprehension that the reader finds satisfying. Nevertheless—and remembering Sir Cyril Burt's humbling admission that "in spite of all the work on eye-movements, speech-habits, brain centres and the like, we still do not know what goes on in the brain or mind of the practised reader or what are the actual processes by which the beginner first learns to gather meaning from the printed page"—we can say that modern oculography at least gives some basis from which to start assessing the relative merits of writing systems. Since the movements of a reader's eyes provide almost the only objective data available for an analysis of the process of silent reading, some basic knowledge of these directly observable symptoms is indispensable if we want to study perceptual differences between readers.

Let us therefore return to the work of Javal. He showed that an educated adult reader divides each line of print into a number of sections of about ten letters each; these sections are seen during a rhythmical series of eye-pauses. The switch from one section to another is carried out in a sharp saccadic movement in the course of which there is no vision. Javal and his colleagues were surprised to find that the number of saccadic movements did not vary with the distance between the reader's eye and the page; hitherto it had been assumed that a reader's eye moved through the same angle for each new fixation, which would have meant that the number of fixations varied with the distance.

Javal's basic discoveries can now be amplified as follows. A reader's eyes do not move smoothly along the lines of print, but perform a series of rapid jerky sweeps, followed by pauses that are relatively longer but still rather too short for ordinary time-measuring instruments. The length of these pauses varies very little with either age or education after the age of five, but remains fairly constant for all human beings. There may also occur a variable number of back-ward glances (called *regressions*) on the same line of print, and a regular backward sweep takes place from a point somewhere near the end of one line to a point near the beginning of the next line. All the eye-movements are so rapid that practically nothing can be registered during the period of time that they take; thus, all import-ant visual impressions must be received while the eyes are pausing. Each of the 'resting' intervals is called a *fixation* (or 'fixation pause'); it lasts only about 0·4 seconds in a very young child, and only 0·2–0·25 seconds after the age of ten years. The movements between pauses are even shorter in duration, and once the reading has become a skilled operation, these movements take no more than 10% of the time spent in reading. It is important to note that all these eye-movements in reading are typically reflex in character: the speed of the motion is not under voluntary control, and once a movement has started, its direction cannot be reversed until after a due pause.

Moreover, as Javal first noticed, during its saccadic motion the eye behaves as if it were 'blind'. That is, the cortical mechanism 'ignores' the blurred sensations on the retina during an eye-movement. Otherwise, as we shall show later, it would not be able to deal with the oncoming package of information received from the subsequent fixation.

Before going into further technical detail, we must draw attention to the close relationship between oculomotor behaviour and the perceptual processes in reading. Eye movements are simply the results of muscular contraction; they are only the observable symptoms of what is going on. Reading, however, is essentially a thought process, whereby percepts are fused into units which yield meaning. One well-established connection between the two kinds of activity is that the rate of comprehension conspicuously drops with the onset of any irregularity in the eye-movements. This irregularity can be caused by the fatigue of certain eye muscles, which usually results after about two hours of reading. However, if a reader has been instructed in making frequent control of his comprehension of the contents, say every half-hour or so, he shows no significant sign of either actual or hidden fatigue even after six hours of otherwise continuous reading. There are other connections, more relevant to the child learner, between oculomotor behaviour and the higher processes of reading. It will be recalled that the rate of comprehension could be calculated fairly accurately in terms of the span of recognition (the amount of visual information received in an average fixation of a reader's eye). Since the duration of pauses varies relatively little, the number of pauses per line of print may be taken as a significant indicator of a reader's perceptual capacity. In this respect there is an important difference between a child learner and an experienced adult reader. A child of six, who is probably near the end of his first year of learning to read English, has to make about three times as many pauses per line of print as does an educated adult, even if all the words are familiar to him in their spoken forms. It is during this year of a child's life that the greatest growth in oculomotor ability takes place. But besides this physical factor there are other influences upon a learner's progress. The fatigue of the visual mechanism that we mentioned above tends to occur fairly soon when the rate of comprehension is intrinsically low, irrespective of general readability factors: the jerky movements became more numerous, and a beginner, unlike an advanced reader, cannot easily counteract the fatigue by periodic checks of his comprehension of the material. At this stage it is the 'lower' perceptual

processes that absorb most of the young learner's energy; this is bound to be so, whatever teaching means and methods are employed. The development of the span of recognition is a longer and more gradual process than most adults realise. Even the acquisition of the necessary degree of visual acuity has been shown to depend largely upon the familiarity of particular objects and shapes: the very recognition of letters and letter-groups develops only with practice.

This inherent difficulty for the learner is likely to be aggravated if there is any further cause of jerky eye-movements such as regressions. Now such regressions are frequently called for in the elementary stages of learning any writing-system, such as CES, in which the grapheme–phoneme relationship is inconsistent. The first viewing of a letter-string evokes an auditory percept which later needs to be adjusted to correspond with a meaningful item from the young reader's auditory stock. For instance, when a reader with a limited span of recognition meets the word *danger*, he will probably respond to the first three graphemes with a phoneme string that corresponds to *dan* (to rhyme with *can*); on reading the next letter, he will have to review the string and alter the last phoneme so that the whole group results in *dang* (to rhyme with *bang*); when he comes to the fifth letter, he has to review it all over again, to produce *dange*, which he may hear either as rhyming with *flange*, or (if he reviews the vowel as well as the consonant) as rhyming with *change*— and heaven help him if he knows *blancmange*! Alternatively, if he perceives the last two graphemes (*-er*) as a group, the total result is likely to resemble—*clanger*. Until his span of recognition is developed to the point at which he can perceive all six letters in one fixation, he will need to make at least one regression, and possibly two or three, before he can attach a meaning to the word.

Some further details about eye-movements were reported by M. D. Vernon. After each saccadic movement the eye makes a more or less fine adjustment to the particular fixation point. The initial error in finding a suitable fixation point does not depend upon the size of the angular shift, but rather upon the distance of the fixation point from the central position of the eyes. The type of adjustment is largely determined by the reader's standard of oculomotor accuracy: if the initial error is relatively large, the adjustment to a suitable point of fixation is usually performed in a series of jerky corrective movements, but small errors are usually adjusted by a 'glide' to the proper point. Moreover, the degree of adjustment and the length of time taken in making it depend upon the reader's need to perceive the printed signs with greater or less accuracy. The young child is thus at a double disadvantage. First he will probably need to make more jerky corrective movements; and of course, the longer the adjustment, the smaller the proportion of time for clear vision. Secondly, being unfamiliar with the shapes of letters, he needs to make a more accurate adjustment after each movement. Thus a child who is given too difficult a task at the early stages of learning to read may be caught in a vicious circle: more saccadic eye-movements are likely to produce more errors, which in turn frequently cause him to perform additional jerky movements, and perhaps regressions. By contrast, once some perceptual skills have been developed, the accuracy of fixation can be significantly reduced; it has been demonstrated experimentally that for an experienced reader the point of fixation need not always coincide with the target, even when the latter is only a single dot. If you consider the highly complicated interplay that must take place between afferent and efferent visual impulses during the process of adjustment that we have described in this paragraph, you will realise why reading must be described as a 'skilled' operation, in the sense in which 'skill' was defined at p. 26, even without the complication caused by an inconsistent writing system.

We can gain more insight into the complexity of perception if we go on to examine the connection between the span of recognition and what is called *short-term visual memory*. Let us start from the fact, which we noted above, that the significant impressions from print are received almost exclusively during eye-fixations, and that during its saccadic motions the eye behaves as if it were 'blind'. It was Raymond Dodge, writing in 1907, who first postulated that the 'blindness' is in fact a manifestation of 'purposeful' functioning of the *central nervous system (CNS)*: the cutting off of the input for a brief period allows "the mental clearing up of these relatively minute perceptual units" before the next batch of impressions is received. Subsequent writers have noted that it appears possible for human beings to perceive events without being immediately aware of them and to store the information for a limited time and to attend to it later. Recent experiments with advanced readers seem to indicate that before the 'clearing' process starts at all, there is a period—it might be called a 'buffer-storage phase'—during which the reader can review any portion of the 'immediate memory' image. In one instance, after the subjects had been exposed to a fairly large group of printed signs for a short period of time (15 to 500 milliseconds), they were able to reproduce any required portion of the group within a period of 0·25 second to several seconds, though they were unable to reproduce the whole group. This kind of reviewing of visual memory images in reading we shall refer to as *immediate inner scanning* (abbreviated as *i.i.sc.*). We choose this term by analogy with the corresponding auditory phenomenon, *inner speech* (*i.sp.*), which also has been receiving increasing attention, especially since strictly behaviourist theories have been superseded, and of which more will be said in the following chapter. *I.sp.* and *i.i.sc.* are alike in the following respects. They are related in the same way to the higher mediating processes in that they both function as a sort of machine for collecting information from the overt activity of listening to speech or looking at a visual display. They both occur, as the names imply, after the particular external stimulation has been discontinued. Finally, just as *i.sp.* is usually much more rapid than normal speech, so *i.i.sc.* is assumed to be significantly faster than overt scanning; this would account for the fact that the smaller the number of eye-fixations per line, the higher is the rate of comprehension.

Also related to *i.i.sc.* is another phenomenon, known as *peripheral vision*, which is of crucial importance to progress in reading. We said above that human beings can perceive events 'without being aware of them'; we can also say that a viewer is not equally 'aware' of all parts of a panorama; he is able to concentrate his attention on one or other detail within it, irrespective of the direction of his eyes. A man driving a car, keeping his eyes focussed on the road directly ahead of him, is still able to attend to the movements of vehicles to his right and left, which he observes (as we say) 'out of the corner of his eye'. The expression is quite an apt one. To explain its significance, we must add to what we have said about eye-movements by giving a brief account of the interior mechanism of the eye itself. The retina of the eye is a sensitive concave screen incorporating a complex system of nerve-endings. Near the centre of this screen is a small depression called the *fovea centralis*; in this area the nerve-endings are most numerous, and have special functions concerned with intensity and colour. The clearest vision results from the stimuli of light falling upon the fovea centralis. Outside this is the area called the *macula*, where the nerve endings are less numerous; light falling upon the outer area of the retina produces what is called *peripheral vision*. Whenever anyone is looking at unfamiliar objects or con-figurations, the process of recognition seems mainly to depend on the *central vision*, i.e. that part of an optical image that falls on the fovea centralis, and little use is made of peripheral vision. In particular this seems to be the case at the early stages of learning to read, as we can tell from the distance between two adjacent points of eye-fixation when an average child is reading: the number of pauses per line indicates that he does not sufficiently 'register' the letters whose optical image falls on his retinal macula and not on the fovea centralis. M. D. Vernon found that at normal reading distance the fovea could contain the optical image from a horizontal line of print only 0·6 cm. in length, whereas the macula could contain the image from a line 6·0 cm. in length. It follows that a child cannot be expected to recognise 'simultaneously', within a single eye-fixation, more than one or two letters of the size usually used in a primer. It has always been assumed—almost intuitively, but correctly—that large letters are more suitable than small ones for the initial teaching of reading. This is so because, as we said above, the acquisition of the degree of visual acuity necessary for reading depends upon familiarity with the shape of the letters; the young reader is unaccustomed to perceiving small shapes having several smaller distinctive features. Letters that appear quite large to a literate adult look small to a child who is still trying to learn them. Print is smaller than you think. (You can check this for yourself. Take out a small coin—a new penny or five-penny piece. Estimate how many letters on one line of the print used in this book you think it will cover. Will it cover the word 'estimate', do you think? Put the coin on the page and see.) A child finds it difficult, then, either to perceive small letters or to see more than one or two large ones at any one fixation. It has been shown that the oculomotor behaviour of young readers even at the moderately advanced stage may be significantly influenced by differences of no more than 20% in the size of letters: 10-point types secured a higher efficiency than the smaller 8-point types. On the other hand, Burt found that "with adult readers enjoying normal vision, wide variations in design, size or measure seemed permissible without greatly affecting efficiency of reading". Larger letters do not improve the rate of comprehension of an educated adult, for they tend to discourage the use of his peripheral vision, and they require a higher number of eye-fixations per line.

The central difficulty for a young reader is this: at a stage when he needs large letters, and is still dependent upon the use of his central rather than his peripheral vision, he can seldom perceive simultaneously a graphemic string that has any semantic value. If he can translate the visual percepts into auditory percepts, he can store them in his short-term memory and recall or review them at the next fixation, for his auditory memory is likely to be better developed than his capacity to remember 'meaningless' visual shapes. A phonemic notation, therefore, provides an aid to the short-term memory; but an inconsistent notation, in which graphemes and short grapheme-strings do not correspond with any definite auditory percepts, makes storage difficult. Even a moderately advanced learner of CES often has to review certain letter-groups when he comes to the end of an unfamiliar printed word, before he can adjust his visual percepts to correspond with a familiar auditory sequence. The process of adjustment, however, is not the same at every stage of learning; it is more difficult for the beginner, who has to carry out an 'overt' review of brief letter-sequences, than for the advanced learner, who can use 'higher' and more economical processes, as well as being able to perceive more letters 'simultaneously'.

Before proceeding, we had better explain the implied reservations about the use of the word 'simultaneously'. Modern researchers have suggested that the mechanism of our visual perception of the external world can be likened to that of a television receiver. The visual 'field' can be imagined as a fine network, the loops of which are filled with sense-data which have arrived in a certain temporal sequence; these data immediately go through a process of elaboration, so that they are not necessarily perceived in the order of their arrival. This process of elaboration and perception at the mechanical level is—judging by the duration of eye-pauses—so rapid that the 'higher' CNS processes function *as if* all the pieces of information obtained during an eye-fixation arrived simultaneously in an absolute sense. Strictly speaking, all perceptual processes depend on the corresponding physiological functions, and are thus time-dependent variables. For our present purposes, however, all the information registered within a single recognition span can be treated as 'simultaneous'. But we may note that the process just mentioned is not confined to the visual modality, and that its relationship to 'higher' CNS processes will be discussed further in Chapter 6. At that point we shall also refer to some quite recent work on oculography, and to the discovery that within each fixation the eyes perform a subsidiary series of very tiny rapid movements, which suggests that even the inspection of a single letter is not strictly speaking a simultaneous process. But for the time being we can usefully continue to think of the eye-fixation as a unit.

Let us now study an eye-fixation record of an advanced reader (Figure 4), one "somewhat better than the typical college student"— at least by the standards of 1928, when Buswell conducted his experiment. The oblique lines indicate the centres of fixations with reference to the reading material. The number at the top of each oblique line shows the serial order of the fixation, and the number below the oblique line indicates the duration of the fixation in units of 1/25 second.

Figure 4: Eye-fixation record of an advanced reader

```
        1              2      3     4      5
not  ᵈark.   The  briǵht  mooᵖ  shoᵖe  in  ᵃt  the
     8              6      6     7      4

        1              2      3   4       5
windoᵂ.   Peter  coᵘld  see  eᵛerytʰing  in/  the
     7              6      3   4       4

        1         2   3     4      5      6
rooᵐ.  All  at  ᵒnce  ʰe  heaʳd  a  noise.  ᵖeter
    7         6   3     8      5      6

        1         2        3          4     5
opeᵖed  his  eyᵉs.  He  saw/that  the  ʳoom  ʰad
      7       4        7          4     3

        1            2          3
growᵖ dark.  Sometʰing  was  oᵘtside  the
     7            6          7
```

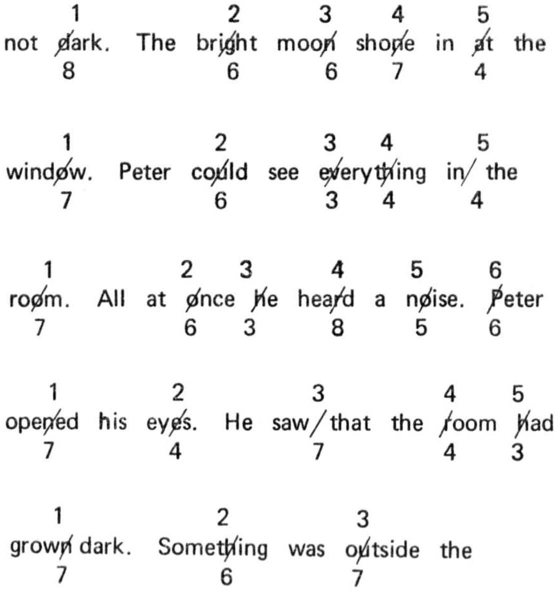

We can use the data recorded here to calculate certain parameters that characterise reading ability. The total fixation-time was 5·36 seconds for 41 words. The total number of pauses was 24 for 159 letters, occupying about 54 cm. of printed lines. Therefore

Average duration of fixation . . . . 0·22 sec.
Average length of print per pause . . . 2·2 cm.
Average number of words per pause . . . 1·65
Average number of letters per pause . . . 6·42

Now, as was mentioned above, ophthalmoscopic measurements have shown that the fovea centralis, the area of clearest vision, only receives an optical image that corresponds to a line about 0·6 cm. long at the normal reading distance of about 30 cm. Buswell's reader evidently took in 2.2 cm. at each fixation. It follows that almost three-quarters of the printed line covered in an average pause fell on the retinal macula, the area of peripheral vision, yet the reader was able to 'recognise' all the words in the text. The converse situation has been described by E. C. Poulton, who found that as the 'window' available to a reader was reduced from a full line to five words, errors increased significantly, "probably as a result of tighter pacing and reduced peripheral vision". From such experiments we may deduce that an advanced reader does not depend much upon his central vision, but makes up for the lack of visual acuity by using at least two distinct perceptual skills. He 'recognises' some parts of the printed matter according to the context rather than by visual perception, and other parts by applying the *i.i.sc.*, that is, by reviewing the graphemic sequences (derived from both central and peripheral vision) that have been stored within his short-term visual memory.

It is this second type of perceptual operation that is particularly important in reading CES, because an inconsistent orthography continually imposes the need of adjusting visual percepts to the familiar stock of auditory percepts. The eye-movement record of Buswell's advanced reader indicates that he could make that adjustment without any significant number of *overt* regressions. This is because he was covering graphemic strings of about six or seven members in a single eye-fixation. The mutual influence of letters with regard to phonemic value rarely extends beyond a five-letter string; an extreme example might be the word *though*, in which the phonemic value of every grapheme remains indeterminate until the whole word has been perceived. The reader who can take in such words at a single eye-fixation must be recognising 'immediately' almost every letter-combination that determines the phonemic values of the constituent members, and he must be doing so by means of the *i.i.sc.* In other words, the process used by an advanced reader would appear to be physiologically different from that used by an average child at the initial stages of learning to read.

This conclusion appears to be supported by the results of some of the very earliest experiments with tachistoscopic exposures. As long ago as 1885, Cattell showed that an advanced reader can perceive an average English word which has been exposed for only 0·125 sec.

Since the average eye-fixation of such readers lasts about 0·2 to 0·25 second, the time of exposure did not allow more than one single fixation interrupted about the middle of its normal course, and the perception must have proceeded mainly on the basis of information received from the retinal macula (see calculation on p. 50). Cattell's description of the experiment seems to imply some such operation as *i.i.sc.* of an image derived from peripheral vision.

The main conclusion to be drawn from the evidence presented in this chapter is that an inconsistent orthography such as CES may be expected to create serious difficulties for an average child before he has developed the experience and capacities necessary for making effective use of his peripheral vision: i.e. general familiarity with printed material; short term storage of impressions from a substantial part of the whole retinal area; the *i.i.sc.* of the information in terms of graphemic strings; and visual memory for such strings until they have been translated into significant percepts, auditory or semantic. We shall of course have to consider whether there is also a corresponding positive influence in CES, in being conducive to a further growth of the visual field after a reader has reached a moderately advanced level of proficiency. The possibility of this growth—the ability to 'see' syllables, words or even phrases as 'wholes'—will be discussed in Chapter 6. The crucial question remains; whether any eventual positive benefits of an inconsistent writing system can be shown to justify all the difficulties that it may have created for an average child by being used too early. It will probably have been used too early if it has been introduced before the child has completed that secondary stage of reading ability at which he can not only perceive and analyse word-shapes but also perceive and analyse word-sounds, and can make systematic relationships between shape and sound. Admittedly, a few exceptionally gifted learners are able to overcome the difficulties of an irregular writing system at a very early age, and even begin to derive from it some benefits that would not accrue from a phonemic notation. But it would appear that the average child is not philogenetically equipped—particularly in respect of visual perception—to gain any advantage from a partly ideographic system before he has mastered some elementary reading skills. This will be even more apparent when we have considered some auditory factors and their interplay with visual phenomena at various levels of literacy.

"Language", wrote C. L. Wrenn, "is the expression of human personality in words, whether spoken or written." Every linguistic activity is influenced by features of the individual personalities involved; and this is as true of reading as of speech. M. D. Vernon, in a report for the Medical Research Council in 1930, noted the subtle interaction between the personality of a reader and his oculomotor behaviour. She found that, other things being equal, the persons who are capable of steady and fairly accurate fixation of an object usually read a line of print in a smaller number of pauses than those who conspicuously lack that capacity. If, however, the reader is interested in a particular text but has some difficulties in comprehending certain words, reading tends to become slower, and there appear some gross irregularities in the number of regressive eye-movements. If the text causes some trains of thought and imagery of no great personal interest to the reader, or some imagery with a mildly affective tone, the reading tends to become very rapid, and the irregularity in eye-movements become moderate. We may deduce from this as well as from later reports that the perceptual processes themselves are influenced by the attitude of the reader towards the material he reads. This may well be true even at the most elementary stage, even before the material in itself can yield much meaning for the reader. Though in this chapter we have written of visual perception largely in technical and impersonal terms, we recognise that in each new learning situation there are many variables and imponderables that arise from the personalities of both learner and teacher. This applies equally to our discussion of other perceptual operations. Any human activity is influenced by emotional and motivational forces, and if we do not attempt to deal with them here, it is not because we underrate them. The process of learning to read may usefully be distinguished from the goal of being able to read for information or pleasure, but in any real-life situation they cannot be completely dissociated. People do tend to learn what they really want to learn. Teachers who keep in mind the goal of pleasurable reading are likely to be eager to alleviate the difficulties that children encounter in the process.

5
The role of speech in reading

If the first major step in the reading process is the perception of printed signs in terms of graphemes, the second is the translation of these visual percepts into other and more meaningful terms. It is about this step that some of the basic disagreements on methods of teaching reading have arisen. Although it is generally accepted that reading properly so called must consist in the ability to derive semantic meaning from visible signs, experts have differed about the 'stepping-stones' towards that meaning, and in particular about the mediating role of the auditory percepts involved. Most writers have emphasised the normal child's need to rely on his experience of spoken language while learning to associate printed symbols with the significates of words. This need is especially evident when the writing system used is an alphabetic one, in which printed symbols basically stand for speech sounds, and therefore can convey the writer's ideas only via some auditory percepts however rudimentary or vestigial. Yet there have been disagreements concerning the use, if any, that ought to be made of these speech-elements during the process of learning to read. What is particularly involved here is not merely the overt activity of reading aloud, but the role of what has been variously called 'silent speech' or 'internalised speech' or 'sub-vocalisation' in the process of silent reading. It has long been known that at every level of literacy some type of auditory or vocal process occurs between the stage of visual perception and that of the full awareness of the meaning.

By the middle of the present century there had emerged two conflicting trends of thought on the place of such auditory elements in learning to read: one insisted that there was no possibility of dispensing with them, the other virtually denied the need for them altogether. At one extreme, a behaviourist school, represented by P. B. Ballard and by Leonard Bloomfield, developed the argument that for all normal children the mechanical response to printed words—i.e. the translation of visual symbols into speech-sounds— is an essential and unavoidable condition of learning to read, and produced the impression that the testing of a pupil's phonic skills provided the best guarantee of his progress. This process was derogatorily called 'barking at print' by some exponents of the opposing view, who held that the development of associative bonds between visual and auditory elements of the language actually interfered with the process of interpreting *written* messages, i.e. with 'reading proper'. According to Buswell, there should be no instruction in oral reading at all, 'inner speech' should be suppressed from the start, and every reference to written symbols in terms of auditory factors should be avoided. More recently it has been maintained by D. Wilcox Gilbert that even a tendency to articulate words in reading is detrimental to the efficiency of oculomotor behaviour and "holds back movements of the eyes". Jagger, writing in 1929, thought that his argument against encouraging the use of 'inner speech' in units smaller than phrases was supported by the fact that congenitally deaf children can learn to read "as cleverly as those whose faculties of hearing are unimpaired". This idea is reminiscent of those of John Wallis (see Chapter 2) and also of the Würzburg school's 'imageless thought' concept; yet it is scarcely helpful in teaching normal children to read an alphabetic system of writing. For it may be that deaf children develop other modalities to compensate in some respects for their deficiency of hearing, and the fact remains that normal children do seem to rely considerably upon auditory percepts, especially at the initial stages of learning to read an alphabetic system. Despite all that has been written on 'internal ised speech' and the like, insufficient attention has been given to the relationship of these phenomena to the systems of writing concerned. Again, too little distinction has yet been made between the function, intensity and effects of auditory percepts in an adult's silent reading of a conventional orthography and the role of these percepts in the early stages of a child's learning to read at all. How to balance the necessity or inevitability of 'inner speech' and its corollaries against the possible adverse effects of its persistence is an important educational problem. Any progress that can be made towards resolving it has a bearing not only upon teaching method but also upon the choice (since choice is now possible) of teaching media for the initial stages.

It should be noted that when the earlier views of 'inner speech' were being formed, two important developments had not yet occurred. In the first place, the role of auditory percepts in silent reading could not be fully assessed, because although their existence was reported on introspective evidence, there were no instruments by which any symptoms of these percepts could be established or measured. In 1959, however, Ake W. Edfeldt of Stockholm described an important series of experiments using highly sophisticated apparatus. He distinguished six stages or degrees of 'inner speech', ranging from the saying or loud whispering of almost every word to a stage at which no symptoms are perceptible to an unaided observer, but tiny movements of the tongue can be registered by electromyography (the recording of electric activity in the muscles). All the evidence suggested that silent speech in some form always accompanies reading. Only in the case of very good readers (such as some university teachers) did the incidence of silent speech ever approach zero, and even with them it increased when the text was blurred or the material exceptionally difficult. Edfeldt found no support for the view that oral reading and silent reading are mutually counteractive processes, and adduced experimental evidence for thinking that they are two forms of the same ability, and indeed that readers at all levels unconsciously resort to silent speech as an aid to reading and to improved comprehension. He noted that most early training in reading would tend to the formation of strong connections not only between printed-text stimuli and oral speech-motor responses, but also between printed text and auditory responses; the phenomenon of 'inner hearing' had, he thought, been too little investigated. This last idea points us to the importance of the second development referred to above: the earlier rival schools of thought on inner speech were established before the concept of the 'smallest significant unit' of this activity had sufficiently crystallised. The notion of the phoneme, and the problem of defining it, though known to linguists, had not engaged the attention of educational psychologists. Yet it is relevant to the central problem of reading an alphabetic system of writing, and especially to the role of speech-elements in that process.

Let us approach it now by way of some points from the preceding chapter. While a child's span of recognition is narrow—i.e. when he can perceive in each eye-fixation only that portion of print whose optical image falls on the retinal area of clear vision—he needs an aid to his short-term visual memory. In order to 'scan' a whole word the average child may have to perform two or more saccadic eye-movements. Moreover, each eye-movement is preceded by a 'clearing-up' process of the visual impressions as such: these impressions must give place to the following batch and therefore cannot be stored in their original form. There is an immediate process by which the sense-data are elaborated into significant visual percepts, the graphemes. But graphemes are difficult percepts to store: they are relatively new to a child, in comparison with percepts of speech in terms of phonemes. For instance, a child at the early stages of learning to read may be able to reproduce a chain of five to ten or more phonemes, even if they represent nonsense syllables; but he appears unable to reproduce a corresponding number of simple printed shapes (having no sound-value) that have been exposed for the same period of time as that taken by the comparable phonemic chain. (A relevant experiment is described in Chapter 8, p. 112). The decay of purely visual percepts appears to take place faster than that of auditory ones. For this reason alone we would expect the average child to have to translate each batch of graphemes into phonemes immediately (i.e. before proceeding to the next eye-fixation) if he is to retain the information until the whole word has been scanned. In any case, a child has normally already learned his mother tongue by listening and talking, and the first stages of his learning to read will tend to be based on his oral repertory. At this stage, therefore, a simple one-to-one grapheme–phoneme relationship is helpful to the reader. But eventually, when the reader's span of recognition has become large enough for the string of graphemes recognised in a single eye-fixation to be translated as a whole into either auditory or semantic percepts, then there is not the same evident need for the grapheme–phoneme relationship in the writing system to be an easy and consistent one.

Here again we must distinguish two stages of the development in reading ability. A learner can be said to have reached a 'moderately advanced' stage when he is able to perceive in each eye-fixation a graphemic string that he can translate, with a reasonable degree of certainty, into the corresponding chain of phonemes. This implies that he must have mastered a set of 'rules' for this translation that are valid for a substantial number of words of the language—or rather, of the writing system that is used for that language. A consistently phonemic notation is, by definition, 'regular' in this sense. In an inconsistent notation such as CES, some words can be regarded as 'regular' (if they conform to any discernible 'rules' in respect of their grapheme–phoneme relationship), and others as 'irregular'; the distinction is further examined in Chapter 7. It is inessential here whether the reader can apply these rules consciously or not, so long as the time taken does not exceed the capacity of the short-term visual memory to hold intact the requisite string of graphemes. But a reader can be considered to have progressed beyond this 'moderately advanced' stage when his rate of comprehension in silent reading is higher than in listening to the same material in a spoken form. It is generally accepted that this higher rate of comprehension is accompanied by (and, according to some investigators, caused by) the elimination or substantial reduction of the intensity of 'inner speech'.

Ideally, therefore, whereas the medium by which reading is taught at the initial stages ought to help the average child to translate the percepts of graphemes into semantic meaning by way of auditory percepts, the system of writing to be used at and beyond the moderately advanced stage should be such as to contribute towards the reduction of inner speech. Since even adults apparently sometimes find it easier to manipulate the percepts associated with spoken language than those associated with the written counterpart, it is small wonder that the majority of children—even at a fairly advanced stage of reading—seem to have to translate a written message into some form of speech before being able to apprehend its semantic meaning.

Now obviously there is a great difference in the facility which various writing systems offer for that translation. A purely ideographic system does not allow any translation into sound unless the reader already knows the meaning of the word in both forms. At the other extreme, a purely phonemic system makes it possible to translate any written word into its spoken counterpart, even if the meaning is unknown, provided that the reader knows the symbols for individual phonemes. Notice, however, that in a purely phonemic notation there is no inherent connection between the shape of written *words* and the sound of their spoken counterparts; there is a definite connection only between individual letters of the alphabet and individual speech sounds of the language. If a child is to learn to read such a system of writing, therefore, he has not only to be able to respond to individual characters in terms of phonemes, but also to learn the perceptual operation of blending individual phonemes into the chains that correspond to morphemes and words, before he can recognise meaningful units in this notation. Anyone who can be properly said to read even the simplest English words, like *sat*, must be able to respond not only to three individual letters but also to the sequence as a whole. This holds good whether he first identifies the appropriate phonemes and then synthesises them, or first responds to the whole sequence and then differentiates it from *cat*, *mat*, etc. As Elkonin has pointed out, the learning even of this type of operation is a major task for a child. But it is a small step in comparison with the task facing a child who has to start learning to read by means of a semi-ideography such as CES, in which sequences of visual percepts often have to be adjusted before they correspond with the appropriate phonemic chains. When the average child uses CES in the initial stages of learning to read, the interplay between his visual percepts from print and his stock of auditory sets must be highly complicated.

For example, at an early stage of learning to read, a child who sees the word *heather* is likely to respond to the two initial letters in terms of the phonemic chain /hiː/; this auditory set will have been established for him by frequent encounter with the pronoun 'he'. In the next eye-fixation, when he perceives the sequence 'heat' or 'heath' his response will be reinforced and confirmed. He is then likely to add the phoneme /ə/, as a fairly frequent response to the final graphemes 'er', and so produce the chain /hiːθə/. He will be able to modify this response into the correct one only if his stock of auditory sets is a rich one that contains a firmly established phonemic chain /hɛðə/, or if he draws an analogy with words like *weather* and *feather*. Otherwise, he is liable to store an erroneous auditory impression, and so to have difficulty in recognising the word when he hears it. This kind of complication in matching auditory to visual percepts arises not simply from the inability to perceive simultaneously more than two or three printed signs, but also from the ambiguities of CES itself. These again give rise to a further type of 'error' resulting from false analogy. For instance, the grapheme-string *heathen* is likely to elicit the response /hɛðən/ by analogy with *heather* and *weather*. The beginner thus faces a double difficulty in reading CES: in any case, by the time he reaches the end of a letter-sequence which is translatable into a chain of phonemes (even a fairly 'regular' one like *stamp*), the initial part of the visual percept may have suffered some decay; in addition to this, in many instances (even simple words like *bath*) he has to review the print and continue a readjustment of percepts until he manages to assemble a chain that fits both the graphemic sequence and one of his auditory sets. A semi-ideographic type of writing system makes it difficult for the average child to reach the point in the process of reading at which he can recognise the spoken counterparts. In a system such as CES the associative bonds that have to be developed for interpreting graphemes in terms of phonemes must be complicated structures which have to perform several distinct operations. Their complicated nature may be realised if we consider merely one feature of CES: the dependence of a grapheme's sound value upon its place in the word and upon the elements of print that follow it. For example the sound value of the grapheme 'a' may vary as follows: æ: in *bat, ballot*; ɔ: in *ball, ward*; ɑ: in *balm, bar, bath*; ei: in *bathe*; ə: in *allot, battalion*. Similarly it could be shown that sound values in many letter sequences are influenced by preceding or following elements in the word. The extent of these interactions can only be fully realised from a study of attempts such as Craigie's to draw up 'Rules of English spelling' (see Chapter 2). As soon as a child starts learning to read English words in conventional orthography, he has to cope with this complicated translation of graphemes into corresponding phonemic chains. It hardly seems reasonable to expect these multiple bonds to develop very fully during the first two or three years of learning to read. Downing and others have shown that we ought not to be surprised in these circumstances if an average child is unable to derive the meaning from print at the initial stage, whatever teaching method be used; and moreover that the difficulties caused by the very nature of CES may limit the reading material effectively available to children, with consequent harm to their intellectual development.

As we have already noted, even when a child has learned the perceptual operations specific to the 'regular' spellings in CES, he is liable to make mistakes whenever he meets an unfamiliar word that is 'irregular'. The extent of this irregularity is often underestimated. The degree of discrepancy between the auditory sets of a learner and the responses actually required could be assessed by making a synopsis of all 'irregulars' in a particular reading vocabulary. It would be possible and useful to extract from a dictionary for moderately advanced learners all the words that deviate from important auditory sets, and to classify them according to the actual phonemes used. One such survey is shown in Appendix B. It is worth adding here that a knowledge of a phonemic notation can be of considerable help to a moderately advanced learner of CES, and that he should be trained to make use of a pronouncing dictionary when he meets an unfamiliar word in CES.

Let us examine a little further the consequences of the fact that

a child learning to read CES soon discovers that there are some graphemes and grapheme strings that correspond reliably with auditory sets and others that do not. The result of this discovery seems to be that he learns to respond to certain letters and certain sequences in terms of an auditory 'blur' rather than of definite phonemes. We shall see later how such 'blurs' may contribute to what Jagger called "the progressive dwindling of inner speech, which is its proper growth". But at the early stages of learning to read, this blurring may interfere with the development of some fundamental reading skills. It certainly deprives the child of the help that definite phonemes would give to his short-term storage of sense-data from print. The exact nature of this 'blur' and the influence that various writing systems may have upon it are not yet fully understood, but we can give some preliminary account of it if we use the definition of *phoneme* given in Chapter 3 above: "the psychological counterpart of the smallest significant unit of spoken language".

The recent work of Roman Jakobson and others has shown that this 'smallest' significant unit in fact consists of a pattern of various cues 'simultaneously' perceived. That is to say, phonemes are determined by a set or 'bundle' of distinctive differentiation features which can be classified according to sets of contrasts such as Vocalic vs. Non-vocalic; Consonantal vs. Non-consonantal; Compact vs. Diffuse, and so on. These simultaneously-perceived sets of contrasts become meaningful, of course, only within the framework of a wider concept of the 'phoneme' such as was originally proposed by de Courtenay in 1885:

Das Phonem = eine einheitliche, der phonetischen Welt angehörende Vorstellung, welche mittelst psychischer Verschmelzung der durch die Aussprache eines und deselben Lautes erhaltenen Eindrücke in der Seele entsteht = psychischer Aequivalent des Sprachlautes.

For a long while the concept of the phoneme as a psychological event received less attention than it merited, though it was found necessary at about the same time both by de Courtenay and by the English neurologist, J. M. Jackson, to explain the transition from meaningful linguistic units (morphemes and words) to 'an articulatory movement, a physical state'. Recently, however, linguists, phoneticians, psychologists and neurologists have shown an increasing interest in the nature of these 'smallest' auditory units and their part in both 'internal' and 'external' communication.

If we regard the phoneme as the psychological counterpart of a distinctive speech sound, i.e. as a relatively stable and uniform representation, on the perceptual level, of a certain 'smallest' segment of speech which, being used instead of another, may change the meaning of a word, then we can say with de Courtenay that this counterpart or representation is gradually developed in the hearer through a process of blending or assimilating the slightly differing but related impressions which are received, amongst others, when the same distinctive sound-pattern is recognised in various phonetic contexts. (It may be noted that in 1935 Twaddell, without accepting a definition of phonemes as psychological events, considered them in terms not of physically related speech sounds but of "recurrent differential relationships".) So we can think of the phoneme as a pattern or schema or complex 'bundle' of the characteristics by which one group of speech-sounds is differentiated from all others, however the phonetic realisations of it may vary. Each bundle includes traces of the physiological activity involved in the articulation of the speech-sound—these traces might be called the kinaesthetic image of the sound—and also traces of the acoustic products of that physiological activity, which might be called the auditory image of the sound. In attempting to explain certain processes involved in decoding print, we are obliged to use the term 'phoneme' to include not only physiological and other observable events, but also all the psychological counterparts of these events. It would be difficult to understand the process of learning to read an alphabetic system if we could not postulate within that process some unit that mediates between visual percepts of graphemes and the semantic units of the language. Whether or not the physiological basis of this unit can be established, it is still possible on logical grounds to infer the existence of some entity like the phoneme in the sense just described.

Now you will recall that we started by talking about the phoneme in a certain specific sense—as an auditory response to a grapheme which is in turn elicited by a letter that stands for a speech-sound. It was further suggested that, if a letter is used inconsistently in respect of speech-sounds, the response is some sort of auditory 'blur'. It now seems possible to explain that blur in terms of an incongruous mixture or unstable combination of features that are usually associated with different phoneme-bundles. To put it another way, a sensation of auditory 'indefiniteness' results from too frequent exposure to printed signs with inconsistent phonemic value. The sensation could be interpreted as an almost random overlap of several different 'phoneme-schemata' (the term used by Lord Brain). Some further insight into the effects of this kind of overlap might be gained from detailed analysis of what we often call a 'foreign accent'. In this case a further contributory factor is the use of the same printed signs to refer to different phoneme–schemata, which leads to inappropriate transfers from one phonetic context to another. A fairly simple instance arises from the fact that in German an initial letter *v* represents the same sound as the English *f*, and the letter *w* the same sound as the English *v*: an Englishman may not recognise a German's pronunciation of the word *Volkswagen*, and vice versa. Again, an Englishman accustomed to pronouncing *café* as 'caffay' will tend to associate the final é in any French word with a phoneme which is common in English but which does not exist in French. This kind of transfer can result not only in an incongruous pronunciation, but also in a significantly different perception of speech-sounds uttered by others. Just as this distorted perception of speech-sounds can cause reduced capacity in oral communication, so the sensation of an auditory blur as a response to the printed signs for one's mother tongue may be responsible for slow progress in learning to read. This would account for some of the frustration and despair experienced by both learners and teachers, especially at the earlier stages of learning to read, when the child's understanding of printed messages and the teacher's measure of that understanding are mainly based on oral responses.

Before a child has developed the skill of using peripheral vision and substituting a perceptual process (*i.i.sc.*) for a number of saccadic eye-movements, he can be helped by a teaching medium in which, as far as possible, individual graphemes consistently represent particular phonemes. Such a medium enables him to go through a relatively easy process of 'operant conditioning', and to learn to respond to print in terms of well-defined auditory percepts instead of an incongruous mixture of phonic elements or merely a blur. When he has reached the stage at which he can 'simultaneously' perceive at least three or four graphemes, even an inconsistent writing system such as CES is less likely to cause a blur, partly because the longer strings of graphemes (such as *-each*, *-ight*) tend to have a more stable sound-value than do the individual members. A moderately advanced reader with a fairly wide span of recognition can use an orthography like CES in spite of its elements of inconsistency, and indeed, as will be shown in the next chapter, may begin to draw some specific benefits from it. But in order to reach this stage, the average child would appear to need the encouragement provided by a notation that enables him to pronounce printed words correctly. Once a child is confident about his pronunciation he can feel that his efforts at learning to read are successful. This approach is more likely to lead him to consider reading not as a frustrating or useless occupation but as a game of discovery, a first pleasurable encounter with books, which will later become "a machine to think with".

It is not our intention here to assess in detail the merits of particular forms of phonemic notation for the English language; we are more concerned with underlying theory and principle, and there are already available several sources of information about the most widely used of these systems. For initial teaching purposes the following two conditions appear to be fundamental. First, the system must follow phonemic principles with regard to the constancy of sound-value of the printed signs. Because of the large member of phonemes in spoken English, some of them will have to be represented either by combinations of more than one sign or by signs that do not occur in the conventional alphabet of twenty-six letters. The important consideration is that each printed sign or group of signs should always represent one and the same phoneme. Second, the choice of printed signs must be so made as not only to satisfy this phonemic principle, but also to facilitate the transfer to conventional orthography at the point when the initial medium can be dispensed with. The initial medium will have fulfilled its function when the learner has acquired the elementary reading skills, such as proceeding horizontally from left to right, blending individual phonemes into the sounds of particular words, attaining a reasonably wide span of recognition, and building up a reading vocabulary that adequately matches his needs.

The 'Augmented Roman' alphabet that is used in the i.t.a. projects was designed to meet these two requirements in the following ways. As the name suggests, it represents some phonemes of English by symbols that do not occur in the conventional alphabet: ɛɛ, ſ, ꙍ, ꙍ, ʒ, ŋ, æ, ɑ, œ, ʃh; others are represented by combinations of symbols: au, ʄh, ʄh, ʄh, ie, ou, ᴡh, ue, oi; some frequent consonant blends are added to the alphabet: cr, sc, tr, cl, str, sn, pl, thr, fr, tr, gr, bl, sp. The transition to CES is facilitated by the carefully selected shapes of the additional symbols; also the combinations of the existing letters correspond to the most frequent rendering of the particular phonemes in conventional spelling. There is one interesting and well-justified instance in which two characters are provided for the same phoneme: z (as in *zoo*) and ꙅ (as in *is*). Another helpful feature of i.t.a. is that each character has only one form; the capitals are simply larger. Thus the learner does not at once have to learn to recognise several different representations of the same grapheme-string—BIG, Big, big, *big*, *big*, and so on—but only one, big. Not only does this facilitate the perception of grapheme–phoneme correspondences, but it introduces the learner by easy stages to the convention (which is not inherent in the alphabetic system as such) that distinctive forms of letters are used at the beginning of certain words or word groups.

The essential requirement is that the initial medium should help the average beginner, as soon as possible, to attribute to the "little black signs on paper" some definite meaning, at least in terms of speech sounds, even with words that he has never heard or seen before. The mere possibility of attributing meaning to printed signs by means of a phonemic notation is beneficial to a child in two related ways: in the formation of a positive attitude towards the activity of reading, and in the development of his vocabulary. From the very first experience of being able to associate a printed sign with a definite phoneme, he is likely to gain the reassurance of a successful activity and a rewarding progress. He can feel that he is on familiar ground, for he has reached a point from which his further progress depends on the spoken vocabulary that he already has. At these less advanced levels of literacy there is a high correlation between scores in listening and in reading. Conversely, the use of a phonemic system at the early stages of learning to read may also help in the enlargement of a child's vocabulary. When a child hears himself pronounce a word that he meets for the first time in print, he begins to develop the corresponding auditory set; and the confidence that the notation is never misleading, and that his pronunciation is therefore correct, will reinforce this development. This can apply even before the child understands the meaning of the words that he utters, for a child who can utter a word that he has read can ask a meaningful question about it. Moreover, as Mowrer said, "information is rewarding for the reason that it helps an organism to prepare for future events". The learner will probably come, sooner or later, into a situation where the word is meaningfully applied, and the probability that he will then understand it increases with his capacity to perceive the phonemic sequence. Thus the word becomes, in Mowrer's terminology, 'associated' with a thing in the 'naming relationship', under which conditions it acquires the capacity to "arouse some part of the total reaction produced by the thing itself." The uttering of a new word is both an expansion of experience and an extension of power.

It should now be clear that the derivation of correct phonemic chains in reading is more than mere 'deciphering', important as that stage is. As Buswell wrote in 1928, "the physiological distinction between reading and deciphering can scarcely be overemphasised"; still less can the distinction at the psychological level. The two processes are nevertheless interrelated. The development of meaningful auditory sets is fed back into the process of reading in two ways: (a) familiarity with the corresponding phonemic chains facilitates the adjustment of visual percepts (as is often required in reading CES), and (b) the more rapid acquisition of semantic meanings, in the ways referred to in the preceding paragraph, naturally increases the rate of comprehension in reading. We show in Chapter 8 how these two claims can be verified by measuring the speed of word perception and the rate of comprehension of groups of children who have been matched in every respect except the teaching medium. We shall also describe experiments to test the hypothesis made in this chapter that an average child has to translate his visual percepts from print into definite phonemic chains in order to help his short-term visual memory. It can be shown (a) that when the translation of unfamiliar printed words or quasi-syllables in a certain system of writing requires complex perceptual operations or, even worse, when no logical operation helps to derive from the visual percept any clear phonemic chain, the task becomes frustrating; and (b) that a fairly phonemic notation helps the child to retain the visual percept from print for a sufficient period of time to express it in writing, even if the percept refers to nonsense syllables. Moreover, the results of these experiments suggest a further and more general observation. A child may experience pleasure in this 'deciphering' of print—even before he has fully mastered the operation of blending together the individual phonemes so evoked—in much the same way as a few years earlier he found pleasure in 'babbling', in mere play with phones or insignificant speech-sounds. "The child's enjoyment of making sounds and hearing himself make them is one of the roots of his subsequent enjoyment of literature written and spoken. From these early moments and throughout childhood he is likely to show again and again his pleasure in the phonetic and syntactic patterns of language" (M. M. Lewis, 1963). Correspondingly, at a later stage, he enjoys the matching of shapes and sounds. The experiments we describe give some support to the view that to denigrate the function of 'deciphering'—i.e. the perception of individual letters (the secondary symbols) in term of graphemes and their translation into phonemes, which are the primary symbols of human communication—in the initial steps towards literacy, is no more justified than to ridicule a baby's 'babbling'. Each is a rudimentary stage in the acquisition of control over language in one of its forms.

Reading, as distinct from deciphering, consists in "making sense out of printed matter". A teaching medium based on phonemic principles contributes towards that end by facilitating the erection of an 'auditory scaffolding' which helps the child to make the fullest use of his oral inventory, i.e. not only his own spoken vocabulary but also his auditory percepts, and so to develop a positive attitude towards literacy and to acquire the elementary reading skills. But this initial teaching medium must be so devised and used as to allow the scaffolding to be removed when it is no longer required. That stage has been reached when the rate of comprehension in reading significantly surpasses that attained by listening. The advanced reader, it seems, can often dispense not only with the perception of letters in terms of individual graphemes but even with any translation into definite phonemic chains; that is to say, he may be able to derive the semantic meaning more or less directly from the visual percepts of print, resorting to a form of 'speech' only when the meaning is difficult for him to grasp without it. Since auditory percepts have normally this lesser degree of importance for the advanced reader, the phonemic notation suitable for initial teaching can be superseded. The introduction of conventional orthography, far from being a regrettable concession to "tyrant custom", is a step forward, and promotes some higher reading skills, such as the perception of larger 'wholes'.

6

The perception of words as wholes

We have suggested that, although a writing system in which the relationship with speech is a complicated one is not entirely suitable for the initial teaching of reading, yet it may be conducive to the development of some more advanced reading skills. This suggestion is not new. Pillsbury and Meader in 1928 pointed out that "the non-phonetic character of English orthography and the habit of seeing masses of letters instead of individual letters operate to restrict the association of individual sounds with corresponding auditory and motor sensations". The reader therefore has to look for the relationships in a graphemic sequence before giving any response in auditory terms. Some other languages have to be read in a similar way: for instance, "in the Russian language the phoneme and its concrete variant, the letter, is determined by position in the word", and "therefore, to designate the sound form of a word and syllable it is necessary to be orientated to the succeeding letter and its sound value" (Elkonin). Two generations ago, eminent English scholars like Henry Bradley, W. A. Craigie and Daniel Jones were pointing out that a good orthography for practical purposes cannot consistently observe purely phonemic principles; that a semi-ideography has several advantages (see p. 26); and that advanced readers are very little disturbed by the discrepancy between speech and spelling, since what they are primarily aware of is the meaning of the message. If a semi-ideography can be shown to afford positive benefits—and in particular if it promotes the integration of visual percepts in reading—one might naturally ask whether it should not continue to be used from the very beginning of learning to read, despite all the difficulties for an average child that we have so far discussed.

Part of the answer can be given by restating Passy's main argument, over forty years ago, for the use of phonemic notation in teaching reading. He bases it on the generally-accepted principle,

69

pedagogically justified, that various kinds of difficulty should be tackled separately. In reading languages like English and French there are two distinct groups of difficulties. The first group stems from the very nature of perceptual processes in reading any alphabetic system—the need for translating visual into auditory percepts; the second is caused by the particular vagaries of traditional orthographies in the representation of speech. Consequently, Passy argued, these two groups of difficulties should be tackled separately in the following way. First of all, some appropriate texts should be rendered in phonemic notation, "as if the French language had never been represented in writing in any other way"; then children should be taught to read such texts, and thus they would master the initial skills "as quickly as Finnish children do in their language". As the second stage of teaching procedure, when children are able to read the phonemic texts with relative fluency, they should be given texts in traditional orthography. As there would be a general resemblance, the children would have no significant difficulties in transferring their basic skills to the new material; after a little initial hesitation, they would soon know how to read conventional spellings.

This reasoning is sound enough, as far as it goes, and is equally applicable to the use of any alphabet specifically designed for the initial teaching of reading to children who at a later stage will have to master a more difficult writing system. But it does not take into account any possible advantages of the conventional orthography, and might give the impression that the transfer is no more than a regrettable necessity, to be accepted merely because it has been impossible to introduce a general spelling reform. To create any such impression would tend to induce a negative attitude towards the transfer, and possibly even a reluctance to learn conventional spelling. But the argument for a two-stage process of learning to read is capable of much more positive support, at least as far as CES is concerned.

There are, of course, different views about what actually constitutes the 'first' stage of 'reading'. Broadly speaking, there are two theories. According to S. A. Kirk and others, a child learning to read normally starts—whatever teaching procedure be employed—by perceiving a certain number of printed words as wholes; the analysis into smaller units, such as syllables and letters, occurs in the following stage; finally, a fairly advanced level of literacy is attained when the reader again perceives printed words as wholes, but in a different way, because he is able to short-circuit many of the percepts and associations that he had laboriously gone through at the earlier stage. Sybil Terman and others, however, hold the view that each unfamiliar word, particularly at the initial stages of learning to read, is seen as a series of letters and syllables; and that by a process of associating these elements of print with their counterparts in speech, and more specifically with the existing 'sound-image' of the word, the learner is enabled to recognise the word as a whole when he meets it in print. The discrepancies between these views are more apparent than real, for they arise mainly from variations of emphasis. Both theories are compatible with the two-stage scheme of procedure for learning to read a system like CES. In Kirk's sense Johnny may be said to have started 'reading' as soon as he can recognise the configuration CORN FLAKES and attach the appropriate meaning to it. In another sense he can be properly said to be 'reading' only when he can, without going through the whole process of association all over again, deduce that the configurations CORK, LAKE and CAKES each correspond to a meaningful item of his spoken repertory. The completion of the real first stage of reading requires the ability not only to distinguish between similar configurations but also to relate those distinctions to speech sounds. In order to tackle a new word, which means a new combination of letters and therefore a new configuration, the child must be able to establish the particular relationship between graphemes and phonemes in that word. This relationship is of course relatively simple to establish in a writing system in which each written sign always stands for one definite phoneme, and thus the first crucial stage of reading is more easily completed. Learning to read CES, however, involves going beyond this. There is a second stage, at which the inconsistency of the grapheme–phoneme correspondence and the consequent blurring effect cause the learner to delay responses in terms of auditory percepts until he has scanned a relatively large unit of print; he is then likely to translate this larger unit as a whole into some familiar phonemic chain. The process of learning to read the word *shoe* or *school* is significantly different from that used to read *hat* or *bell*. This delay of response eliminates the slower perceptual process involved in translating individual graphemes into individual phonemes. Thus it can be said to contribute to the 'Gestalt factor': "a condition favourable to the experience of wholeness".

"To apply the gestalt category," wrote Konrad Koffka, one of the leading exponents of this school of psychology, "means to find out

71

which parts of nature belong as parts to functional wholes, to discover their position in those wholes, their degree of relative independence and the articulation of larger wholes into sub-wholes." In this book we are concerned with reading English words. In most human experience, of children and adults alike, whether speaking, listening, reading or writing, words are parts of functional wholes. We are aware of them only as parts of sentences, or of utterances of delight or surprise or reproach or sympathy, or simply as the 'stuff' that gives us stories or poems or information. Words are usually perceived, if at all, as parts of patterns or structures; their significance inheres in their relationships, like the notes of a melody (to use the classic 'Gestalt' example) or the steps of a dance. Again, each occasion on which any word is used is part of other patterns, made up of all the previous occasions on which that word has occurred in the experience of both the user and the recipient. To develop all this would take us into realms far removed from the topic of this book. We are simply reminding ourselves and you that language, like all living things, is part of an infinitely complex pattern within which many relationships function simultaneously and interact continuously. Yet at the same time, each word does have some degree of relative independence, some 'wholeness' in itself—and especially so when the learner reader encounters it in a written form. In applying the Gestalt category here, we are mostly concerned with the articulation of words as larger wholes into sub-wholes, and with the ongoing process by which the learner reader perceives the larger wholes.

We have spoken so far of three major 'steps' in the process of reading. The first is the perception of print in visual terms; the second is the translation of visual information into some auditory percepts; the third is the derivation of semantic meaning from the auditory percepts, a 'step' which at the elementary levels of literacy is essentially the same in reading as in listening. Beyond this there seems to be a further stage, reached by only the most accomplished readers, at which the auditory elements, though still present, are so reduced in intensity that the reader apparently derives semantic meaning 'directly' from visual percepts. But at this point we must remember that the idea of 'steps', though convenient, may be misleading. The very concept of 'Gestalt' implies that "the total pattern participates in every local reflex, and the idea of 'chain reflex' is a fallacy" (Flanders Dunbar), and that the 'wholes' of operational mechanisms are "irreducible to linear deduction" (Jean Piaget). The 'steps' that we have distinguished are not like paces towards a distant objective, but more like steps in a dance, recurring in new combinations, and meaningful only in relation to each other. The complicated interplay of visual, auditory and semantic elements is illustrated in the following chapter which we call 'Steps in Learning New Words'. If we bear this in mind, however, we can usefully try to specify the 'minimal wholes' at each stage of the reading process— "the functional units of each level of organisation" (Osgood)—and to see how different systems of writing affect that organisation.

At the visual level, a minimal whole (*visual minimal*, or *v.m.*) is the smallest unit which can be 'translated' into either auditory or semantic percepts. Thus a *v.m.* may be either a single grapheme or a graphemic string. Another important category at this level is the *simultaneously perceived whole* (*s.p.w.*), which we define as a percept which has been structured, for the purpose of 'translation', from the bits of information received during one eye-fixation. The reasons for the choice of this unit will be explained in the next paragraph. At the auditory level, a minimal whole (*auditory minimal*, or *a.m.*) is either a phoneme or a phonemic chain corresponding to one of the above visual percepts—a *v.m.* or *s.p.w.*, whichever is the larger; it will vary according to the reader's stage of development at the visual level. At the semantic level, the minimal whole (*semantic minimal*, or *s.m.*) is, by definition, invariably a morpheme. It will be seen that any attempted specification of the functional units in reading is bound to be dependent on two variables: the nature of the writing system, and the level of literacy already attained by the reader. This implies the possibility that any given writing system may have different organisational effects at different stages of learning.

Before proceeding, we offer two reasons for selecting the period of an eye-fixation as an important parameter of the specification of *v.m.* or *s.p.w.* In the first place, you will recall that the most stable factor of oculomotor behaviour in reading—which in turn is highly symptomatic of the perceptual processes—is the duration of an eye-fixation. In combination with the time taken to read a number of lines of defined width, this factor can be used to estimate fairly accurately an average interfixation span, i.e. the length of a printed line that is 'seen' during an eye-pause, for any given reader. Now this interfixation span itself is a variable which significantly depends upon a number of factors, including mental age, legibility of the material in several respects, and also possibly the teaching methods that have been used. So if we were to take groups of subjects,

73

matched in all other respects, and ask them to read the same text in different codes, such as CES and IPA, then differences in inter-fixation span might reasonably be attributed to the code itself. If these differences are taken in conjunction with the rate of comprehension, it should be possible to measure the difference in the average size of units that are 'simultaneously' perceived (i.e. the *s.p.w.*) in each code. The second reason against attempting to analyse the 'gestalting' process within any period shorter than an eye-fixation would involve such philosophical questions as whether a reader's attention "wanders faster than his eyes", to which answers could only be given at present in terms that relied more upon intuition and subjective judgement than upon any measurable factors.

This does not mean, however, that 'gestalting' processes may not be taking place within the single eye-fixation span. Indeed, there is every reason to suppose that they are. In Piaget's words, "toute genèse part des structures antérieures pour en construire de nouvelles et toute structure comporte ainsi une genèse, ou une regression naturellement sans fin (sans 'commencement absolu')". How far back can this regression be explored? Not very far, perhaps. But at this point we may take note of some of the very recent work on oculography to which we alluded briefly in Chapter 4. A research team headed by Egon Guba, starting from the investigation of the oculomotor behaviour of television viewers, has shown that in addition to the well-known sweeps and pauses, the eyes also perform a large number of 'mini-movements'. The number of these movements, considered in conjunction with the total time taken in reading a line of print, suggests that a beginner reader must cover each letter with several lots of eye-movements. For instance, to 'recognise' the letter *b*, an infant has to inspect separately the straight vertical stroke, the circle, and the side of their connection; similarly he finds that the letter *d* is composed of the same elements but that they are connected on the opposite side. By a process akin to 'operant conditioning' the elements and their relatives are 'gestalted' into the corresponding graphemes, so that the child no longer needs to inspect or identify the component parts. The building of this kind of perceptual structure is what Piaget calls non-additive and irreversible. The graphs prepared by Guba and his team show that the number of 'mini-movements' performed by the eyes significantly depends on the I.Q., and it is therefore conceivable that the process of 'grapheme-gestalting' takes longer in the average child than in exceptionally-gifted ones.

Another line of thought is that graphemes may be perceived in much the same way as was suggested in Chapter 5 for the perception of phonemes—i.e. by discrimination of various features within a total pattern rather than as separate and distinct units. It has been pointed out by Watmough that when phonemes are broken down into their inherent distinctive features, that is, into their ultimate discrete signals, the number of such contrastive distinctions is quite small—certainly smaller than the number of phonemes—as they can be combined and permuted in different ways. Similarly, graphemes are formed out of a relatively small number of simple shapes, most of which have already been used in the existing alphabets. We may note that an alphabet of 26 letters has an advantage, purely at the visual level, over a phonemic notation for a language which has 47 phonemes, since a smaller number of graphemes requires a smaller number of combinations of discriminative features, and the perceptual processes at the visual level can be correspondingly faster. Enlarging the alphabet results in a slower reaction time at this level, though of course this may be more than compensated for if the additional symbols help to accelerate higher perceptual processes. The role and significance of 'mini-movements' of the eyes may prove to be highly relevant to the choice of writing systems for various purposes. Meanwhile we can make use of the concept of 'minimal wholes' to develop the proposition that each writing system plays a different role in the processes of 'gestalting' in reading and in learning to read.

In a pure ideography a $v.m.$ is always a single grapheme which directly corresponds to a semantic whole, which also corresponds as a rule to a phonemic chain which is therefore the $a.m.$ Before anyone is able to read such a system, the process of integration at the visual level must invariably have reached the equivalent of a semantically meaningful unit. The difficulty of learning to read a pure ideography is not only that many complex visual percepts are required but also that there is no possibility of using an auditory 'scaffolding' in terms of individual phonemes. At the same time this means that 'inner speech' in terms of subvocalising individual graphemes is not responsible for retarding the eye-movements at any stage of literacy, so that an $s.p.w.$ of about two graphemes, once it has been attained, secures a fairly high reading rate.

In a purely phonemic notation a $v.m.$ is also invariably a grapheme; but in this case it is a relatively simple visual percept and is also immediately translatable into an $a.m.$ of a single phoneme. Thus the structurising at the visual level can be performed in relatively small steps, the product of which can be stored in terms of auditory percepts before reaching a visual whole that corresponds to a morpheme. At the same time, a *v.m.* with these characteristics will tend to bring 'inner speech' into relative prominence, with the concomitant effects that we have described in Chapter 4.

Before we proceed to considering the effects of a semi-ideography, it is worth noting that, as Spieser pointed out, an alphabetic writing, *qua* system, does not provide any symbols to indicate links between the elementary units of print. These links are indicated by other conventions that are not inherent in the alphabet itself: for instance, in English, but not in all languages, it is generally understood that the letters are read in a sequence that proceeds horizontally, always from left to right, and that the spaces between the letters of any one word are smaller than those between words. Thus an 'ideal' alphabetic system—phonemic notation—though highly conducive to the development of associative bonds between individual graphemes and individual phonemes, does not by itself promote the blending of these smallest units into any larger wholes. This matters little when the child is unable to perceive simultaneously more than one or two letters; indeed, it makes it easier for the child to learn to follow the print systematically in the conventional left-to-right order. By contrast, a system like CES sometimes requires minor reversals of this order: in a word like *show*, the second and fourth letters operate backwards, as it were, signalling from right to left. Thus in a semi-ideography, which does not provide a one-to-one relationship of a grapheme with either a phoneme or a morpheme, a *v.m.* is usually larger than a single grapheme. Before he can make use of inner speech, as we know that he does, the reader must take into account a *combination* of the smallest visual percepts; it is these combinations that are the visual minimals. The number of such combinations in a semi-ideography is not as large as the number of characters needed in a pure ideography, but it is considerably larger than the number of graphemes in a purely phonemic system. The reader is required to orientate his attention towards groups or sequences of letters rather than minimal units of print, and thus to perceive within a single eye-fixation a graphemic string that corresponds to a unit larger than a phoneme, though it may be smaller than a morpheme. (An extreme example is a word like *thorough*, which affords no usable auditory or semantic unit until all eight graphemes have been processed.) At a very early stage, the learner has to cope with two classes of difficult percepts: at the visual level there are wholes that do not correspond to single units of print, and at the auditory level there are wholes that do not correspond to spoken words. Even after a child has mastered the elementary skills required for reading an alphabetic script as such, he will not easily be able to grasp why an adult attributes definite speech-sounds to certain letter-combinations. After the simple left-to-right procedure and simple association of grapheme and phoneme, he has to acquire the skills of accepting data from peripheral vision, of using the *i.i.sc.* to assist the short-term visual memory, and of responding to larger groups of signs rather than to individual letters. Beyond this again, as we have said, are other wholes, each providing the reader with some contextual clues; among the most relevant are his oral repertory, and his familiarity with and interest in the type of material that he is reading, which in turn are mutually related to the depth of his comprehension. But within this total pattern of the reading experience, one of the factors is that the rate of comprehension is influenced by the size of the units that are simultaneously perceived. So we must consider whether a semi-ideographic system of writing exerts a positive influence by actually promoting the skill of perceiving larger wholes, and try to ascertain whether, with children who have already developed some elementary reading skills by using a more phonemic notation, CES can in fact contribute towards a better rate of comprehension.

Let us review some characteristic features of CES. Very few of the letters of the alphabet are used with any degree of consistency to represent only one sound. Many sounds have to be represented by combinations of letters, and these combinations again are not consistently used. Some letters and letter-combinations are more ambiguous than others: for consonant sounds, *f*, *j*, and *sh*, for instance, are relatively reliable, while *c*, *g*, and *gh* are unreliable; for vowel sounds, no single letter is unambiguous, but certain combinations, such as *oi* are relatively reliable. The longer the combinations, the higher the degree of consistency is likely to be. The combination -*air* is highly reliable, as also is *ai* followed by any other letter; -*tion* is another consistent combination. Again, vowel quality is often indicated by a retrospective signalling device, such as an *e* at the end of a syllable, which has to be understood as relating to a letter two or three places before it (i.e. to its left), as in *hope*, *paste*. Final consonant groups may give similar signals, as in *path*, *halt* (as compared with *pat*, *hat*). A complicating factor for the learner is that the spellings of some of the commonest words use some of the most ambiguous or unusual combinations: e.g. *you, one, they, there, where, who, women, mother, want, does*. At an early stage of his encounter with CES, a learner will have discovered that the spelling of some words is 'regular' (i.e. resembles that of a number of other words in his experience) and that of others is 'irregular' (i.e. conflicts with that of others that he knows). Now it is evident that to tackle successfully even a 'regular' word like *pate*, the reader has to perform a number of distinct perceptual operations, and that these are likely to result in the translation of grapheme sequences, rather than of single graphemes, into corresponding auditory percepts. But the high incidence of 'irregulars' has an even stronger effect in conditioning the delay of auditory responses until the reader has scanned the whole word. If the reader responds to such words (for instance, *wand*) according to analogies that hold for 'regulars' (*walk, water*; or *band, hand, stand*) he finds that at the end of the process he has to modify his auditory percepts before he can associate them with any word he may have heard before. So in order to avoid unrewarded effort he tends to develop the habit of delaying the auditory response to certain units of print, even in cases where the response might have been a correct one. He is being conditioned, that is, towards perceiving 'structured units' rather than minimals.

Along with the inconsistent grapheme–phoneme relationship—and partly as a product of it—CES has other features conducive to the perception of structured units and to the reduction of inner speech. The English language includes many sets of *homonyms*—words that are alike in form but different in meaning. In some sets (e.g. *bay*, or *pole*, or *seal*), though the words differ in meaning, they correspond in both spelling and pronunciation, and therefore need not concern us here. But there are also two special subgroups: *homographs*—words which have the same spelling for different semantic meanings, but different pronunciations (e.g. *bow, row*); and *homophones*—words which have the same pronunciation for different semantic meanings, but different spellings (e.g. *fair, fare; thrown, throne*). These two sub-groups appear to promote certain 'higher' reading skills in somewhat different ways.

Since homographs are the same at the visual level but may stand for two different word pronunciations, the process of operant conditioning would discourage the formation of strong associative bonds between the graphemic string and either of the possible corresponding phonemic chains. This is, in part, simply a special case of the general effect of an inconsistent spelling system: i.e. that the reader may be forced to change his auditory percepts if his first response is an unsatisfactory one. But in the case of homographs, since the different auditory percepts evoked by the graphemic string *row* (for instance) may both correspond to meaningful items in the reader's oral repertory, he has to distinguish between them at the semantic level before he can adjust his auditory perception of the word. That is to say, he has to make use of contextual clues from larger structures: from the whole sentences and from his comprehension of the whole passage. We may note here that similar considerations apply in the case of two-syllable words whose meaning and function vary with a change of stress, such as *content, compact, refuse.* It is their place in a syntactical and semantic structure that provides the clue to their pronunciation.

Homophones tend to discourage auditory responses in another way. The spelling, being distinctive, provides a more reliable stepping-stone to the semantic level than does the corresponding phoneme or phonemic chain. If the reader translates the word *eye* into /aiː/, the auditory percept opens the way to a greater variety of referents than does the graphemic string. *Rose, rows* and *roes* are more readily distinguishable at the visual than at the auditory level. It is probable therefore that the reader with some experience will tend to short-circuit the usual elementary reading procedure, and to associate the visual percepts of such words more directly with the appropriate semantic meaning. The occurrence of a large number of homophones thus contributes to the progressive dwindling of inner speech and to the corresponding skill to 'structure' at the visual rather than at the auditory level. Moreover, it is quite conceivable that the influence of homonyms of all kinds is extended to the perception of all printed words: at the beginning of any graphemic string in CES the reader cannot be sure whether or not it stands for one of the types of homonym just described, and therefore he will tend to delay his auditory response until the semantic meaning emerges. This possibility awaits more systematic investigation. A full list of English homographs was compiled by W. W. Skeat in 1882, but no comparable list of English homophones seems to be available. A short list is given in Appendix C of this book. In view of the possibility that this feature of CES may influence the perception of words as wholes, it might be profitable to examine and classify a wide range of instances, with a view to their planned inclusion in material for use at appropriate stages of reading progress.

We have indicated some of the ways in which CES, if used at the right stages, might provide the stimulus for learning to structurise larger wholes at the visual level, and thus for attaining the stage at which silent reading yields a higher rate of comprehension than oral reading or listening. Two main points should have emerged about the reading of an imperfectly phonemic or semi-ideographic system of writing: (i) that there is greater need for the skill of *i.i.sc.*, and (ii) that certain features of the system may require the skill of inhibiting auditory responses to certain graphemes or quite long graphemic strings. We must briefly survey the psychological background to these points.

In general terms, it can be said that "all behaviour is energised by drives" (Hebb) and that "to perceive and to know is one of the most important drives of all organisms", leading to the "organisation of sequences of unit acts into instructive, habitual or insightful patterns of responses" (Madsen). Moreover, "motivation is linked to perception almost as closely as it is to learning" (A. J. Laird); and, "no matter how improbable it may seem, all behaviour is response to a particular situation designed to secure the maximum of gratification and minimum of pain" (A. C. MacIntyre). In accordance with these principles, we can reasonably postulate the existence of various 'drives' at work in the learner reader, all conforming to the general tendency of organisms to learn the perceptual processes that are most economical in a particular activity, and each of them influenced by various factors, including the system of writing.

The first group of drives that might be supposed to be influenced by the use of a system like CES is the group promoting the development of the skill of *i.i.sc.* The influence can be partly interpreted in terms of eye-muscle fatigue. At the early stages of learning to read, an inconsistent orthography imposes more regressive eye-movements than a phonemic system. Since each saccadic eye-movement represents a period of practical blindness, it follows that the greater the number of these movements per line, the less is the amount seen in a given time, and the smaller the reward in terms of information per unit of muscular energy. Moreover, a larger number of eye-pauses requires an increased amount of acceleration and retardation of the angular shift, which may be one of the chief sources of the additional eye-muscle fatigue. The basic cause of regressive eye-movements is the need to adjust visual percepts to familiar phonemic chains; in order to avoid eye-muscle fatigue, the reader unconsciously attempts to make that adjustment during each particular eye-fixation. The more difficult the adjustment, the greater the need to complete it within the duration of one fixation by means of *i.i.sc.* CES will thus tend to stimulate the development of this skill, provided that the use of this system be introduced at a stage when the rewards in terms of increased comprehension outweigh the deterrent effects. A child faced with it too early may well find the perceptual tasks over-powering and may develop an aversion towards all printed matter. He will be 'ready' to broaden the range of his peripheral vision only when he has become familiar with print in general, and confident that it makes sense. This he can best do through the use of a phonemically consistent writing system. One of the most important features of the i.t.a. programme has been the demonstration that children are 'ready to read' this kind of script at an earlier age than they are the conventional one, and so master the basic skills sooner. But there comes a stage at which we could expect the learner to be stimulated by the specific 'cognitive dissonance'—the discrepancy between speech and conventional spelling. Such a "discrepancy between belief about a situation and perception of that situation acts like a drive. The subject acts to reduce the dissonance by either withdrawing from the incredible situation or by changing his beliefs" (J. McV. Hunt). Face a child with CES too early and he may with-draw from it; prepare him properly for it, and he is likely to react to the transfer as a fair challenge. Indeed, the 'fairly advanced' reader is one who finds it easier to recognise print in terms of fully meaningful visual percepts than by the assiduous employment of auditory minimals which is encouraged by a phonemic notation. One of the main conditions for this simultaneous perception of larger wholes is a well-developed *i.i.sc.* skill. Its benefits include not only a reduction of eye-muscle fatigue and of wasted physio-logical energy, but also a faster reading process at the visual level. The product at the semantic level—i.e. the rate of comprehension—is related both to the *i.i.sc.* and to the inhibition of auditory responses.

The second group of drives that we are considering are those that concern this skill to inhibit. In general terms again, inhibition in many forms is now known to be an integral part of the activity of the central nervous system; and "conditioned inhibition" is "a habit of ceasing to respond in a particular way in a particular situation". An increasing amount of information is becoming available about the mechanisms that might be responsible for various types of inhibition and facilitation; but little of it has yet been applied to problems of reading, or showing how certain degrees of inhibition may take on a facilitating role in learning. We offer some tentative suggestions.

The development of a mechanism that inhibits auditory responses to individual graphemes could also be interpreted in terms of physiological fatigue. Inner speech, though it is useful in learning to read, and also at later stages when the material is difficult, involves some expenditure of physiological energy. Edfeldt's researches are based upon this fact, and, as he pointed out, the theory that silent speech might be merely a redundant accompaniment to the reading process "does not agree with what seems to be the wisdom of the body as regards the conserving of energy". It is conceivable that, when even a single phoneme is perceived as a result of 'translation' from any writing system, there is a characteristic 'reverberation' in the nervous system for a brief period of time, as well as an excitation of the assembly cell responsible for the particular 'phoneme-schema'. Reading is quite accurately regarded as a form of work. The translation of individual graphemes into individual phonemes requires some output of energy; and if it be attempted in relation to an inconsistent writing system, with many 'irregular' spellings, much of that effort is unrewarded. It does not agree with "the wisdom of the body". We might reasonably expect that under the influence of a phonemically inconsistent writing system a moderately advanced reader will learn to delay auditory responses to ambiguous units and so reduce the intensity of inner speech. When Buswell said that "readers who move their lips in silent reading lose the advantage of rapid fusion of words into ideas", he was perhaps putting the cart before the horse; but it seems to be true that the 'fusion into ideas' is closely related to the size of the units in which subvocalisation takes place, and if the reader can deal 'simultaneously' with groups of phonemes, the interference between visual and semantic levels is reduced. A writing system that tends towards the extinguishing of motor or auditory responses to individual graphemes or to small grapheme-combinations is helping to free the reader from strict temporal sequences. It is stimulating him to move towards that advanced stage of 'gestalting' at which, even in written form, "a single sentence in language, as in music, is perceived nòt in real time, the few seconds that it occupies, but simultaneously, as a unit" (Whatmough).

The translation of print into auditory percepts should therefore be considered as only one of the operations that are indispensable for the average child. The aids for that operation should be replaced, as soon as possible, by those that tend to promote 'higher' reading skills such as the perception of larger wholes. Different stages of reading ability are best served by the use of different teaching media. Future research is likely to be most profitably directed towards establishing the right points of transition from one medium to another. But there need be no question of regarding CES as a regrettable and out-dated nuisance that must in time be generally superseded. Far from it. Besides all its often-asserted merits—its historicity, its preservation of etymologies, its serviceability in representing equally well the various dialects of spoken English, its world-wide diffusion, and the vast treasures of literature already committed to it—it has positive educational advantages: it contributes to the elimination of responses to print in the limiting terms of separate phonemes, to the reduction of the intensity of inner speech, to the development of structured visual percepts, and so to that increased rate and depth of comprehension that makes the very using of it a reward in itself.

Of course the learner himself need not be aware of this process of conditioning. "In reading what attracts attention, what finally comes to consciousness, is the idea. The elements are added in the process of understanding rather than in the perception of words alone" (Pillsbury and Meader). Even after the process has been completed, the improving reader may not notice how he has moved from reliance on a temporal sequence of events (the auditory responses) to a simultaneous perception of visual units that yield semantic meaning more or less directly. What matters is that the teacher should be aware of the nature of the processes that are taking place—almost miraculously, it may seem—in her pupils.

7
Steps in reading new words

We can now study more closely the effects that the semi-ideographic character of the English writing system may have upon the visual and auditory imagery of a learner. The majority of letters in CES have no unique phonemic value; hardly any individual sign in the alphabet can be expected consistently to elicit the auditory image of a definite phoneme. Rather, at the early stages, there seems to occur a sort of auditory 'blur' resulting from the mixture of various phonemic elements. The effect of this blurring is that the learner will tend to attribute meaning not so much to single letters as to certain groups or classes of letter. The less definite the phonemic value of single letters, the stronger the significance of the group or class. Learning is, in a sense, searching for definite patterns—"Man seeks patterns for his comfort" (W. Grey Walter)—and when the search is frustrated by the inconsistency of single items, the group or class will attract the greater attention. What then are the dominant patterns into which letters can be grouped in CES?

The classification is of course unconscious most of the time. As is often and rightly pointed out, one is normally unaware of the separate processes in reading. Moreover we are dealing here with abstractions, in much the same way as we have discussed the phoneme as an abstraction—a recognition of sameness in certain sounds, or the perception of recurrent differential relations. Just as in ordinary conversation we can ignore many acoustic facts of speech and perceive only phonemic features, so we can sometimes ignore certain other characteristics of speech sounds and make a second degree of abstraction in terms of 'vowelness' and 'consonantness'. This generalised distinction is a basic and unconscious one, which is made very early in a child's experience of language.

If we consider first the letters a, e, i, o, u, y, as they are used in CES, we can recognise that in the vast majority of cases they stand for speech-sounds with a high degree of sonority and of what

Jakobson calls 'chromaticity'. Although these characteristics of the sounds are difficult to describe, a young child obviously 'feels' them and is able to imitate them. The means by which he is able to recall and reproduce the sounds with these characteristics might be called the 'image' of the group of sounds. Under what have hitherto been the usual conditions of learning to read CES, it is the image of these characteristics, rather than of definite phonemes, that first becomes associated with this class of letters. These six letters become (in Osgood's terminology) 'assigns' of vowel quality but not at first of any particular speech-sounds. This particularisation comes later, when relationships within letter-sequences are perceived. The visual perception of any of these six letters in CES tends to elicit first the same partial response, an auditory image of 'vowelness'.

The creation of such an associative bond is promoted by the high mean frequency with which this class of letter occurs. The following computation can be drawn from a table compiled by Fletcher Pratt. Of each 1,000 letters used, in a variety of texts, 400 are of the above class; i.e. their representation is 40%. But these six letters constitute only 23% of the alphabet; on the average, each is likely to occur about twice as often as any of the other twenty letters. This proportion of letter occurrence correlates highly with that of vowel-phonemes. G. Dewey found that of each 100,000 phonemes occurring in a range of varied texts, 38,000 are vowels; i.e. the representation is 38%. If we also remember the great variety of vowel-sounds in English, we realise not only the high frequency of their occurrence as a class, but also the indefiniteness with which they must be represented by means of only six letters. In the following pages, the response to these letters by the auditory image of 'vowelness' will be represented by the symbol θ. The contrasting image, a response in terms of 'non-vowelness' will be shown by the symbol $-$. This contrast seems to be the basic pattern of the child's discrimination of speech sounds, and of their associated letters. Only later comes the identification of specific consonantal letters, and later still that of the vowel letters.

Evidently, other recurrent differential relations are perceived in speech, and gradually become associated with corresponding unconscious classifications of letters or letter-groups. The drive to perceive and know impels the learner to find patterns in the relationships between sequences of graphemes and chains of phonemes. In this chapter we suggest that it may be possible and useful to discern certain sets, each consisting of a relatively small number of visual symbols, that facilitate the formation of patterns and the tackling of new words in an economical way. It will also be shown that the formation of such patterns will at first lead a moderately advanced reader into some errors of pronunciation when he tackles certain types of unfamiliar word. If, however, these likely errors can be predicted, their retarding or discouraging effect can be avoided or minimised.

A moderately advanced learner of CES (as defined in Chapter 5) will probably have learned to associate most of the letters of the alphabet with the consonant sounds that they usually represent, and the other six letters—rather less confidently—with certain kinds of vowelness. At this stage, in reading unfamiliar words, he apparently performs four perceptual operations, which we shall describe in the order in which they seem usually to happen. In each operation there is assumed to be a stimulus and response, which we refer to as S_1, r_1, S_2, r_2, and so on. But there is a great deal of interplay between them, including feedback between the operations, as well as an imponderable influence of some larger contexts, and the total time taken may be very small. The temporal sequence is in any case largely conjectural, and is merely assumed here for convenience of exposition.

We wish to stress that the analysis we offer here, though it is based on the theoretical considerations presented in the foregoing chapters, and supported by actual observation and experience, is not put forward dogmatically. It is rather a working hypothesis, and it is capable of being tested in many learning situations, both inside and outside the classroom. Indeed, such testing, and consequent modification in the light of greater experimentation and fuller theory, is of the very essence of the procedure we are recommending for the teacher of learner readers.

Operation (i) is *the perception of the word as a whole and the discrimination of the letters according to their classes.* On encountering an unfamiliar word in print, a moderately advanced learner of CES performs first a rapid scanning, and registers only the classes of the letters in the sequence. He will have discovered from previous experience that further registration of individual letters cannot be relied on until he has taken account of some other characteristics of the whole sequence; if he uses the details to translate individual graphemes into phonemes before he has arrived at the end of the word, he may have to revise the auditory percept. So, if only to secure an economy of perceptual operations, he develops the habit of scanning the whole sequence first. Thus, for instance, the word *rancid* as S_1 will evoke the pattern of images –θ--θ– as r_1. In this particular example he will probably at once be able to assign specific consonant values to at least three of the letters, and the correct vowel quality to the two letters first perceived as θ. But in the case of some other words, he will have to register, even at this stage, some characteristics of various classes of letters. It is not possible here to give an exhaustive list of them, but the following are some of the characteristics that seem usually to be discovered at the earlier stages of learning to read.

The learner soon distinguishes the letters that consistently correspond to definite consonant sounds from those that do not. The letters *f, j, v, x* and *z* have a high degree of reliability. So (once he can distinguish them) have *m* and *n*, except in a few words like *autumn* and *solemn*; *k* is also consistent, except in a few common words like *knee* and *know*. The four letters *b, d, p* and *q* may at the early stages be confused because of the general similarity of their shapes; but, once correctly perceived, they can be fairly confidently translated into phonemes, at least until the learner begins to enter the adult world that involves words like *debt, doubt, queue, receipt* and *psychology*. A group that represents a further degree of unreliability includes the letters *s* and *t*, not only because their sound value as single letters is uncertain in intervocalic positions (as *basin, nasal; fatal, nation*), but also because they may combine with other letters (especially *h*) to represent yet other sounds.

Two other classes of letters seem to be distinguished by the relative beginner. The sounds that are represented by the letters *l*, *r* and *w*, and by the letter *u* when it follows *q*, are easily articulated after the majority of other sounds, and in some words they almost disappear in medial or final positions, as in *finger, grow, calm* and (in some regional pronunciations) *almost*. This characteristic of these letters can usually be perceived as a contrast to the other letters that may stand for English consonants, or to the same letters occurring initially. The image of this contrast will here be represented as $+$. So the word *window* as S_1 will tend to evoke the pattern $-\theta--\theta+$ as r_1, the word *library* $-\theta-+\theta-\theta$, and so on. Frequently (depending, it seems, on the teaching method that has been used) *r* and *w* may be perceived in some words only in relation to a preceding vowel (as in *thorn, gown*); in this case the learner has already gone on to the second of the four perceptual operations that we are describing.

The other classification likely to have taken place in the subconscious mind of the learner concerns the letters *c* and *g*: they are the least reliable consonant letters in CES. Their sound-value varies not only when they occur singly in any position, but even in combinations, such as *ch* (*change, ache, school*), *gh* (*ugh!*) and *ng* (*finger, singer, singe*). The learner begins to recognise such patterns as that, when followed by the letters *a, o* and *u*, they are usually pronounced as k and g, but that the letters *e, i* and *y* 'cause' them to be pronounced as s and dz. (Even then, the exceptions include many common words like *get* and *give*.) If the learner is to make any pattern here for his comfort, it can only be by the discovery that in words like *case, gorge, gum, cease, George, giant, gymnastic,* the vowel that follows *c* or *g* has a retrospective signalling function as well as standing for 'vowelness'. The first group of vowel letters (a, o, u) standing in these positions will be represented as $\theta_{\backslash}$, and the second group (e, i, y) as θ'. This perception of the interaction of letters leads us to consider the next stage, in which the product (r_1) of the first operation, along with some other clues, becomes an important stimulus (S_2) for the second operation.

Operation (ii) is *the perception of letter grouping and its significance, and of the role of letters in certain positions*. The learner will have noticed, even before he starts attempting to read, that the vowels are the nuclei of spoken words, and more particularly of syllables. As he learns to read, he transfers that role of vowels to the corresponding group of letters, the six 'assigns' of vowelness. Somewhat later, but before attaining the moderately advanced stage, he discovers that the pronunciation of these letters that stand for vowel-phonemes largely depends upon the position in the syllables and upon their relation to other letters. Again the 'drive to know' impels him to seek analogies in letter-groupings.

A common instance of this is the effect of the final *e* in words like *care, make, bite* and *hope*. The moderately advanced reader is likely to be so inured to this effect that his r_1 might be represented not as $-\theta-\theta$ but as $-\theta-*$. This, acting as S_2, will tend to result in a long diphthongal vowel as part of r_2 to such words. He will go on to notice a similar retrospective effect of final o or y in words like *polo, baby, lady, tiny* and *fury*; but he will further discover that in these cases it does not occur when the r_1 pattern is $-\theta--\theta$, as in *lotto, tabby, tinny, furry, funny* and *hurry.*

Other complex patterns of r_2 can be traced. Whereas the words *habit, livid, haven, tiger* will all evoke the same r_1 $-\theta-\theta-$, they are likely to be differentiated at the r_2 stage. The learner may conclude that in such words it is (oddly enough) the final consonant of the *second* syllable that seems to have the determining effect upon the vowel of the *first* syllable: that whereas most final consonants seem

89

to indicate that the first vowel is a short monophthong (as in *habit*), yet several letters seem to have a different influence, so that the first vowel is a long diphthong (as in *haven*). This latter effect is usually associated with the final letters *l*, *m*, *n*, *r* and *s* in contrast to other consonant letters. For instance we have *tabor, taper, tiger, token, tonal, toper, totem, tribal, iris, minus* as against *tabard, tablet, tacit, rigid, timid, tonic, topic*. True, there are exceptions (*talon, tenor, travel*), but they seem to be so relatively few as to count as 'irregular'. Now, this assertion is one that we invite readers to test out for themselves. One way of doing it is to invent some words on the above pattern and decide how you would be most likely to pronounce them. How would you pronounce *traver*, for instance, or *tiban* or *hevis*? And why? You would probably be influenced by the analogy of words that happened to be uppermost in your mind (perhaps *travel* or *quaver*). The learner too will be influenced by the words of similar pattern that he has met most often in speech and writing. If we can discover such patterns and analogies, then we may be able to anticipate his reactions to new words. We may note here that this problem in reading CES is not alleviated by the use of a phonemic system for *initial* teaching. Even if a child knows that *tiger* is the same as tieɡer, and that *timid* is the same as tʃmiɖ, this knowledge does not help him with the pronunciation of the word *tidal* when he first encounters it in CES.

The image of the letters *l*, *m*, *n*, *r*, *s* in the final position operating as above can be represented as }, and that of other consonants in the final position as (. Again it may be noted that these images include not only the consonant-phonemes associated with the letters, but also an awareness of a relationship between these letters and something that has preceded them.

We have given only two examples—one obvious, the other less clearly discernible—of the kind of image-pattern that may emerge from a developing experience of CES. It would of course be possible to list many more. The result would be as complicated as the so-called 'rules' of English spelling, to which in some ways these image-patterns are related. But we are not here concerned with 'rules' in any prescriptive or even conscious sense, but with discovering what in fact does determine a learner's responses to series of graphemes—the analogies that rightly or wrongly he is likely to draw for himself.

The longer the word, and the more inconstant graphemes it contains, the more indeterminate will be the r_2—i.e. the less indica-

tive of the pronunciation. Thus *molten* and *solder* will both elicit
$-\theta\vdash -\theta-$); *futile* and *pumice* $-\theta- \theta-*$; *cyclonic* and *cyclamen* $-\theta -\vdash\theta -\theta-$,
and so on, which may lead either to the 'received pronunciation' or to
an error. It is seldom possible to predict error on the basis of such
responses unless we also compare the structure of each unfamiliar
word with that of the words most frequently encountered by the
learner previously.

Operation (iii)—perhaps the most important of all—is *the
distribution of the degrees of prominence within the word*. Before a
child starts to read at all, he is aware of some patterns of prominence,
or stress, in spoken sequences. As M. M. Lewis pointed out,
"children first attend to the intensity and duration of speech". Such
features of speech are called 'supraphonemic', i.e. they have no
reference to specific phonemes as such. In other words, a child can
learn them even before the significant sounds of the language.

Neither in CES nor in most writing systems are there any
symbols to indicate the degree of prominence or stress to be given to
different parts of a word. Nevertheless, a child learns very soon to
transfer to his oral reading the supraphonemic features of speech.
When he does so, he has taken the significant step of attributing to
the print something which is not indicated by any individual grapheme, nor by any arrangement of graphemes. This kind of learning
is explicable only by the normal circumstances of learning to read
one's native tongue. As soon as a child starts to vocalise written
words, he begins to associate the patterns of prominence in familiar
words with the corresponding parts of their written forms. The
rhythms of spoken language assert themselves as soon as he reads
aloud. When he reads words like *baby, mother, family*, he 'knows'
that the first syllable has a greater prominence than the second. This
partly explains the fact that a child will soon be able to distribute, in
the majority of cases, the correct degrees of prominence in quite unfamiliar letter sequences. It is one of the chief reasons why a young
child needs to be spoken to, read to, and sung to, even in words
that he does not fully understand, and to be encouraged to imitate
these activities. Speech, song, poetry and dance are all contributing
to his experience of rhythms, and preparing him to recognise
familiar stress-patterns in written words. When he comes to read
the words *nation, ration, fashion, ovation*, he may err in respect of the
phonemes, but he will seldom be wrong in distributing the stress.

The moderately advanced reader is often at a loss because he
cannot attribute the correct phoneme sequence to a string of

graphemes until he has identified the pattern of stresses. For instance, the same sequence of six letters is differently pronounced in *nation* and *nationality*. The longer word can be uttered only when it has assimilated itself to the familiar rhythm of words like *personality, electricity,* even *international*. The learner reader comes to the stage at which he needs to ascertain the appropriate degrees of prominence for the letter groups in new words. This, together with r_2 becomes S_3. Thus the sequence of letters in the word *pertinacity* elicits the same r_2 as that of the word *personality* (i.e. $-\theta\!\!\!\!/ -\theta -\theta- \theta -\theta$), which in turn (as part of S_3) will eventually evoke the same r_3, which can be shown as $-\theta\!\!\!\!/ -\theta -\theta- \theta -\theta$. The horizontal lines under the class-symbols represent the degrees of stress: full line for strong, interrupted for secondary and dotted line for weak.

There is no doubt that such an example of r_3 represents "a very complex pattern", as M. M. Lewis puts it, in which "rhythm, stress, variation of pitch and variation of sound groups are all elements". If you consider the large number of children who fully master the mechanism of reading such words, whatever the method by which they are taught, it does seem that there is some innate capacity of the human mind to perceive such patterns and to relate them to visible symbols which in themselves do not indicate them. "Feeling for the sound and rhythm of verse develop before the meaning of words" (A. F. Watts). This feeling can only gradually be associated with written symbols and with the percepts of graphemes and phonemes. The learner will sometimes make mistaken associations. It is worth investigating whether these errors can be predicted. To explore this possibility fully it would be necessary to use another set of schemata: patterns of images representing the distribution of degrees of prominence in English words. The formation of these patterns in the learner would seem to depend not only on his inborn capacities, but also on his reading age and vocabulary, which in turn depend on many factors in his previous experience of language both spoken and written. Even a pragmatic analysis of such patterns might help to explain how and why a moderately advanced learner will use analogy appropriately for many words that are not familiar to him. For instance, he is likely to stress the word *cachinnation* in the same way as *combination,* $-\theta- -\theta -\theta -\theta\theta-$, *cardinal* as *gardener,* $-\theta\!\!\!\!/ -\theta -\theta\!\!\!\!/$, *certificate* as *magnificent* $-\theta- -\theta- \theta -\theta-(-)$, and so on. This certainly calls for explanation, since there are no symbols that indicate these stress-patterns.

On the other hand, a moderately advanced learner is quite likely to put the same stress in the word *dubiety* as in *certainty*, despite the differences of letters and sounds, and despite the equally available analogies of *variety* and *society*. A possible explanation is that the syllable *dub-*, with its two 'reliable' consonant letters, exercises a determining influence at the beginning of the word. In other instances it may be that the learner pays less attention to individual letters, registering only their classes and grouping in a provisional way. But when he stresses the word *allege* like *alley* or *college*, or *duet* like *dual* or *suet*, he may be using analogy (logically, though inappropriately), or he may simply be following unconsciously the predominant English stress pattern for two-syllable words. The important point is that in many English words, it is only after the learner has correctly distributed the stress that he can assign the correct phonemic value to letter-groups.

Operation (iv), then, is *the recognition of the phonemic sequence as a whole*. Having distributed the degrees of prominence to the groups of letters in an unfamiliar word, the learner can complete the decisive distinction between the letters, scanning their shapes and functions more accurately. This does not necessarily require any overt action such as a regressive movement of the eyes. More probably he uses several perceptual processes 'simultaneously': by means of his central vision he registers the finer graphemic differentia that enable him to translate clear groups of graphemes as required; by means of his peripheral vision he perceives the essential larger patterns; by *i.i.sc.* of both sets of information stored in his short-term memory, he now completes the translation of the whole into phonemic terms. The product of all the previous operations (r_3), together with this inner scanning becomes the stimulus (S_4) for the final response, which is the reading of the word.

For instance, the letter-sequence *certificate* has provided the clues for all the elements for r_3 in the term$_S$ –θ⫽ –θ– θ –θ–*. The letters of the word will thus be scanned in the four units cer tif i cate. The pattern *ce* will tend to elicit the phoneme s, and *-er* the phoneme ə; by contrast, the pattern *ca-* in the last unit will elicit the phoneme k, and the pattern θ–* the phonemic sequence e i t. The unit with the strong stress *-tif-* will elicit the phoneme i for the vowel letter, whereas the unstressed i will elicit a slightly modified phoneme for the same letter at its second occurrence. Finally there will probably be some adjustment of the vowel-phoneme of the final syllable as the reader assimilates the word to an item of his passive spoken vocabulary.

93

Upon such analysis it might be possible to base predictions of a learner's likely reactions to new words encountered in reading. But it should be noted that schemata of this kind are more likely to be used when the word is unfamiliar in all the units provided by the first three operations. On the other hand, if one of the units is 'known' to the learner, perhaps from its occurrence in another often-used word or group of words, he is likely to use the phonemic sequence of that 'known' part. The first analogy that the graphemes suggest may have such a strong effect as to disrupt the usual patterns of reading unfamiliar words, even though the patterns are there to be found. For instance, even when the word *copious* elicits the r_3 –θ –θ θθ), the learner will probably have 'recognised' an analogy with the words *cop, copy, copied, copying*, and will therefore tend to pronounce the units co pi as in the last three of these words. A similar disruption of the pattern might be expected in *tedious*. But if such misleading analogies do not occur to the reader, he will probably use the same schema as for *various, devious, glorious, furious* and so on. Similar explanations could be given for errors in the oral reading of many other unfamiliar words, and are therefore important if we wish to predict or forestall error. There is little doubt that the learner will at first mispronounce the word *gunwale*, because he not only recognises (correctly) the first part, but also thinks (wrongly) that he recognises the second. The pronunciation of *agate* will be influenced by the patterns of *gate* and *again*; *mangy* by that of *man*; *vineyard* by that of *vine* and by the analogy of *graveyard, coalyard*, etc.; *schism, schist* and *schedule* (in the usual English pronunciation) by that of *school*, and so on. Of course these are remote examples; but similar effects are produced by many words that will be encountered by an enterprising ten-year-old. What we are recommending is that anybody who tries to assist the progress of a moderately advanced reader should try to recognise the schemata that the learner is using, so that teacher and learner can make purposeful use of the discrepancies that arise from them.

It should not be supposed that such predictions could equally well be made on the basis of considerations at the syntactical level alone, relevant though they are; Lee's investigation on this basis in 1960 does not support such a claim. Nor is the observation of overt behaviour alone sufficient, though it is certainly helpful. For the prediction of linguistic behaviour, an analysis of inner responses is also needed, and a study of how the stages of perception in general can be related to the perceptual processes required in the reading of

CES. It is obvious that these processes cannot be based on mere rote memory: they are too swift, too complex and too economical. Progress in reading must also be based on principles of economy. In an attempt to elucidate some of these principles with respect to single words, we have suggested a possible analysis into four operations. We must repeat that the suggestion is tentative, and that in any case the interaction of the four operations is continuous, complex and often very rapid. But at least the use of this kind of analysis provides a frame within which we can study the actual responses made by learner readers to some of the difficulties posed by CES. The remainder of this chapter describes one such experimental study and its results.

One obvious method of verifying the hypothesis that learners' errors due to CES are predictable is to carry out some experiments in which groups of subjects read series of words, more or less unfamiliar to them, for which the possibilities of mispronunciation have been assessed in advance. The conditions of the experiment we describe necessitated the presentation of the words as discrete items in a list, i.e. without any meaningful context. It is not possible to assess what bearing this factor may have had upon the attitude or performance of the testees. What was being investigated in this instance was not comprehension but pronunciation, i.e. overt responses in terms of phonemes. Of the words included in the list, there is only one whose pronunciation could have varied according to its function in a sentence, and in fact it occasioned no error at all. If this restricted experiment is otherwise sound in principle, it needs to be followed up by similar tests based on responses to words in continuous passages of prose or verse.

In compiling the list of words for the test, two major factors were taken into account: the average reading age of the subjects, and frequency of word usage. As the experiment was carried out with children in the top classes of junior schools, words with a frequency of usage lower than 20 per million were considered as unfamiliar. This assumption was based on a recommendation of Thorndike (1952) and the consequent limitations of its relevance had to be allowed for.

Each word was analysed according to the series of perceptual operations described in this chapter. If the spelling gave clues which would lead to the 'standard' pronunciation (as given by Daniel Jones's *Pronouncing Dictionary*, 1963 edn.), the word was classed as 'Regular'; if the spelling led to any other phonemic sequence, the word was classed as 'Irregular'. For instance, the word *certificate*, as explained above, gives clues for each of the four perceptual operations which lead to the recognition of the 'correct' phonemic sequence, even if the meaning of the word is unknown. Similarly, words like *slapstick* and *pipkin* lead to processes which seem to follow sets of analogies between CES and the received pronunciation, and they can therefore be put on the list of Regulars (R's). On the other hand the likely effects of the graphemic string *attorney* can be traced as follows:

Operation i   θ--θ)-θθ
Operation ii   θ- / -θ) / -θθ
Operation iii θ- / -θ) / -θθ
Operation iv   at / tor / ney
               æt tɔ ni

Children who perform operation (iii) purely on the basis of spelling will thus be led to pronounce the word incorrectly as to both stress and phonemic sequence. Only those children who have ever heard the correct distribution of stress in this word will be able to disregard the usual pattern; only those who have also heard and noted the specific phonemic sequence used in this word will be able to produce the received pronunciation. Similarly, the word *fulcrum* will produce 'regular' clues only as far as operation (iii); then the moderately advanced reader will probably 'recognise' the letter-sequence *ful-* as used in *fulfil*, and so will pronounce it incorrectly. These two words are therefore put on the list of Irregulars (IR's).

Since the nature of the tests required the oral reading of every word, the list was kept shorter by 10% than those used for graded vocabulary tests, and so was planned to include 90 unfamiliar words. But to make it easier for individual children, it was decided to introduce several words which might be known to particular groups; these words were taken in roughly equal numbers from the R and IR categories and with as low a frequency of usage as possible. In compiling the list as a whole, it was important to ensure that a sufficient proportion of R's and IR's could be matched both in numbers and in frequency of usage. Finally, the words for testing were so selected as to represent a fair sample of different patterns for each of the four perceptual operations. The list was arranged for convenience as shown in Table A; R's and IR's are in alternate columns, but this arrangement is concealed by the disregard of alphabetical order and of frequency of usage.

Table A: Testing list of unfamiliar words

The words underlined are the selected group of 40 referred to in this chapter.
Those with an asterisk are the selected group of 40 referred to in Chapter 8.

Cigar	Aisle*	Baffle*	Allege*	Bidding*	Attorney*
Slapstick*	Phaeton	Badger	Athens*	Birch	Foliage*
Blunder	Triumphant	Babble*	Trochee	Boiler	Duet
Pipkin*	Sceptic*	Behalf	Ballot*	Chart	Dubiety
Cargo	Copious*	Cane	Tablet*	Dibble*	Equity
Bradley*	Signet	Cherish	Impugn*	Brim	Docile*
Cavalry	Worcester	Chant	Fuchsia	Chick	Dromedary
Bully*	Shew	Char*	Ousel	Certificate	Heathen*
Cardinal	Gillyflower	Childish	Elegiac	Boar	Fulcrum*
Compact	Pursuivant	Conductor	Agate	Confession	Pumice
Constable	Vineyard*	Clip	Schist*	Clash	Gunwale
Pratt*	Chasm*	Prescribe	Cachinnation	Potter*	Otiose
Tress*	Stanchion	Trickle*	Cassia	Tucker*	Alibi*
Shelve*	Cyclamen	Sherbet*	Prestige	Sheen*	Pique*
Pout*	Solder	Patchwork*	Mangy*	Pebbly*	Persuade

The tests were performed in 1963–1964, mainly by English children (boys and girls in about equal numbers), selected from the top classes of two London junior schools with somewhat different characteristics. In School 'A' a relatively strong emphasis in teaching to read had been laid upon 'phonics'; in School 'B' no particular preference had been given to any one method of teaching to read. 36 testees were selected from each school on the basis of high Reading Age, as indicated by Schonell's Graded Reading Vocabulary Test, checked against data provided by the teachers. For details see Table B.

Table B: Selection of testees on basis of high R.A.

SCHOOL	'A'	'B'
Age of Children	9.2 – 11.9	10.2 – 11.3
Reading Age	9.6 – 14.2	9.7 – 14.4

To aid analysis of the results, the testees were divided into groups of twelve according to their Reading Ages, as shown in Table C.

Table C: Division of testees into R.A. groups

R.A. GROUPS	I	II	III
School 'A'	14.2 − 12.7	12.5 − 11.3	11.2 − 9.6
School 'B'	14.4 − 13.1	13.0 − 11.6	11.5 − 9.7

Before each testee was asked to read the list aloud, it was explained that this was a test not of the individual child or his knowledge but of the difficulty of words. If the child hesitated for more than ten seconds before attempting any one word, some brief additional explanation and encouragement was given; this seldom needed to be repeated.

A survey of the main numerical data yielded by the experiment is given in Table D. The basic findings are numbers of errors in reading different categories of words. It is apparent that the number of errors in reading IR's is about ten times larger than that in reading R's. The four columns show the data from four different comparisons of the results. Column 1 relates to all words in the list (45 R's and 45 IR's). The other columns relate to specially selected groups of words. As was mentioned above, the criterion for the degree of familiarity of words used in the experiment was related to their frequency of usage. Owing to the lack of more accurate sources, this frequency had to be taken as that indicated by Thorndike and Lorge, which is principally valid for American schools. It was hoped that the consequent possibility of false results might be reduced by taking IR's of higher frequency than R's. From the whole test-list a group of 40 words was selected so that the mean frequency of usage (f_m) of IR's was 6·56 per million, while that of R's was only 4·5 per million. This group of words was again divided into two sub-groups of twenty. Column 3 shows the data concerning the items of lower f_m, i.e. ten IR's and ten R's with f_m of 1·62 and 1·21 respectively; column 4 shows the data concerning the items of higher f_m, i.e. ten IR's and ten R's with f_m of 11·5 and 7·3 respectively. As the last line of Table D shows, the difference between the Means of Errors in IR's and R's is statistically significant in each of the four groups. In simple terms, a 1% *level of statistical significance* means that the same

Table D: Survey of the main data from the test in both schools

Items under Consideration :	1 All 90 words	2 Group of 40 selected words	3 Sub-group of 20 words with lower f_m*	4 Sub-group of 20 words with higher f_m
Sum of Errors				
in 'R's'	193	103	62	41
in 'IR's'	2,190	929	522	407
Mean				
in 'R's'	4.29	5.15	6.20	4.10
in 'IR's'	48.66	46.45	52.20	40.70
Standard Dev.				
in 'R's'	4.65	4.59	5.57	3.05
in 'IR's'	19.14	17.29	14.29	17.44
Standard Error of Difference	2.94	4.05	@ 18.26	@ 14.83
(@ for N 15) 't-test' Value	15.11	10.197	2.52	2.46
Level of Stat. Significance	1%	1%	5%	5%

* f_m stands for the mean frequency of word usage per million.

result could be expected to occur by sheer chance only once in a hundred trials; at 5% level, the chance would be one in twenty, and so on.

Even more important results emerge when the numbers of errors committed by each of the six groups of children are analysed. (See Figures 5, 6, 7 below). The R.A. Group I from School 'A' made no error at all in reading the 45 R's, and the corresponding group from School 'B' made only seven such errors; but each of these groups made about three hundred errors in reading the 45 IR's. Children with lower reading ages made more errors in both categories, but the increase in errors with lower reading age is more marked for R's than for IR's. This tendency is also noticeable in the results for the selected group of forty words and for the two subgroups of twenty words. It may be noted that the proportion of the total number of errors in IR's to that of errors in R's is higher in School 'A' (which placed more emphasis on 'phonics'), even though the children there made fewer errors in IR's. A good many of the words occasioned a similar number of errors in the two schools, as is shown in the scatter-diagrams at Figure 8 below, though the similarity is more striking for IR's than R's. The correlation between schools and reading ages indicated that errors in IR's do not vary so much with different teaching methods or different R.A.'s as do errors in R's. The coefficients differed more widely in School 'A'.

Figure 5: Incidence of errors in both schools

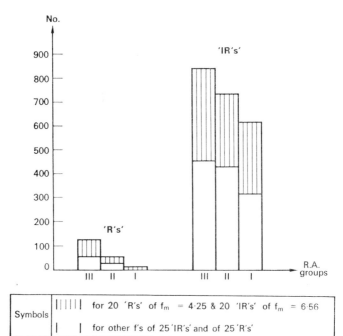

These findings must be interpreted with caution, and they certainly point to the need for further enquiry. The fundamental finding is the significant difference between scores for 'Regular' and 'Irregular' spellings, as they were defined. The hypothesis that moderately advanced learners would be capable of deriving the appropriate phonemic sequences from 'Regulars' but not from

Figure 6: Incidence of errors in School 'A'

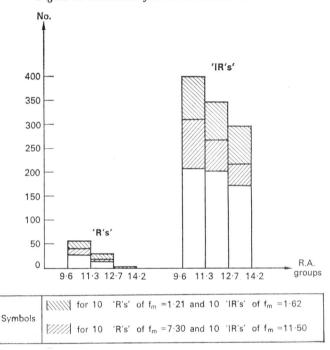

| Symbols | $\boxed{\text{N}}$ for 10 'R's' of $f_m = 1 \cdot 21$ and 10 'IR's' of $f_m = 1 \cdot 62$ |
| | $\boxed{\diagup}$ for 10 'R's' of $f_m = 7 \cdot 30$ and 10 'IR's' of $f_m = 11 \cdot 50$ |

'Irregulars' is in general supported by these figures. An important feature of the results is certainly the similar distribution of errors in the two schools. The product-moment coefficient of correlation between errors for IR's in the two schools is also significantly higher than that for R's; in other words, the errors in IR's were not only more numerous but also more systematic in their incidence. We can at once draw two relevant conclusions. (1) There are certain English words which the learner at certain reading ages is likely to mispronounce on the basis of their spellings, and these spellings can be considered truly irregular and misleading. (2) The occurrence of error caused by such irregularity can be predicted with an acceptable degree of statistical significance. Moreover, if we relate the method of prediction used here with that used in other investigations (such as W. R. Lee, 1960), this second conclusion can be extended to (3) the difficulty caused by irregular spellings can be discovered with more certainty if the previous learning of the child is sufficiently taken into account.

Figure 7: Incidence of errors in School 'B'

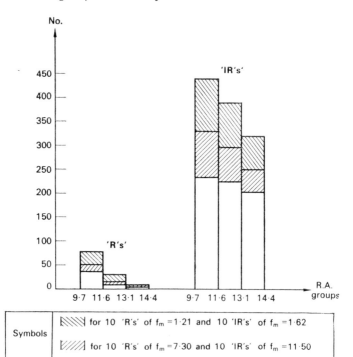

This extension can be developed if we analyse the performances of children of various reading ages in this experiment. The children in Groups I (i.e. 33·3% of the total tested) committed only 7 errors in reading R's, i.e. only 3·6% of all the errors of this type. Naturally this superior performance can be partly attributed to their richer vocabulary—but not entirely, since these groups committed 27·7% of all the errors in IR's. The possibility of a specific coincidence (i.e. that these children actually happened to be more familiar with the

Figure 8: Correlation of errors in Schools 'A' and 'B'

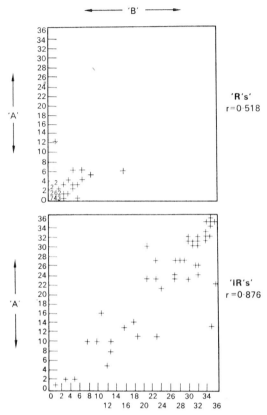

particular words on the list of R's) can be virtually ruled out, since the difference of scores is equally significant in respect of the groups of selected words in which the mean frequency of general usage of the IR's is about 30% higher than that of the R's. Again, similar comparisons of the performances of Groups II and III make the explanation in terms of vocabulary alone appear highly improbable. Group II were superior to Group III in reading both categories of words; but the superiority was more conspicuous in reading R's than in reading IR's. These considerations seem to converge towards some further possible inferences. (4) A higher Reading Age means, among other things, a greater capacity to use analogy in deriving phonemic sequences from spellings. At a higher Reading Age, there is no increase in the number of errors made in reading 'Regulars', however low their frequency of usage; but the capacity to use analogy does not by itself significantly influence the number of errors made in reading 'Irregulars'. One interesting detail of the results is that in reading R's the children of Group I in School 'A' did not make a single mistake in their 540 trials in this category. From this admittedly limited evidence, it would be possible to infer that (5) training in 'phonics' seems to contribute towards promoting the capacity to use analogy in deducing pronunciation from CES.

These inferences, and especially the two last, must be accepted with caution. Their validity may be questioned on three main grounds. (a) There was no direct measurement of the vocabulary range in the strict sense. It was not possible to check whether or not individual testees were familiar with every word on the test list. Indeed the investigation required the use of words from different ranges of familiarity, from a few words supposed to be known to almost every child tested, up to about twenty words which would be unfamiliar to even the most advanced child in the relevant reading-age groups. The familiarity of the words had to be estimated on the basis of Reading Age and the vocabulary of the books used in the school; the test results could be controlled only in the light of word-counts which have limited value in Britain. (b) A relatively small number of words were submitted to testing. The possible combinations within the four hypothesised perceptual operations are obviously far more numerous than those represented in the list used. There are therefore several more questions to be asked. How would the same groups of testees react to other combinations in CES? Are the tested instances sufficiently representative of the system? What is the proportion of 'regulars' and 'irregulars' in the normal experience of children of any given age, ability or background? Is any pattern discernible in the types of error made in the pronunciation of any irregular word? (There are several possible ways of mispronouncing *attorney*.) What would have happened if the words had been dictated, and the testees asked to write them down? These questions indicate the third and most important reason for regarding the findings from any one such experiment as inconclusive: (c) There are at least two sets of variables that are being investigated, one relating to the children and the other to the words used; and the relationship between them is itself conjectural. The test material includes two or three words that might arguably have been differently categorised, according to the analogies which they might be supposed to evoke. The very classification into 'Regular' and 'Irregular' is bound to be related in some degree to the reader's previous experience of CES. Part of the investigation that still remains to be done concerns the aptness, for specific Reading Ages, of the criteria used in defining 'regularity'. Each of the four postulated operations needs to be further examined by specially designed means. The results could contribute not only to greater accuracy of prediction, but to a better understanding of the phenomena involved in learning to read.

Nevertheless, even in the present state of such enquiry, any teacher can make use of the methods adopted in this experiment for the prediction and analysis of error. Whatever measure of success she has, the effects on the learner will at the least not be harmful. The essence of the procedure is that at the beginning of any reading task, the teacher should try to note the words with 'irregular' spelling, and why she believes them to be irregular, and should then note the reactions of her pupils to them. When she has been able to confirm or modify her own predictions for a number of systematically recurring errors, she will have discovered which words can be learnt by unconscious analogy, and which words need special introduction. Perhaps the most valuable outcome of such a predictive approach may lie in its effects on the teacher's attitude. The more she discovers reasons for the blunders which a learner systematically (albeit unconsciously) commits, the more are the negative impacts upon her reduced. The dismay that might be caused by a frequent dissonance between an expected response and the one actually perceived can be largely eliminated. To that end alone, it is worth attempting to analyse the learner's reactions to the vagaries of CES. The learner, too, can be encouraged through the wise foresight that sometimes prevents him from falling into errors, and sometimes enables him to make good use of them. There is good reason to believe that this kind of error-analysis, which is already used in the teaching of English as a second language, is not only possible but profitable in the teaching of English-speaking children.

The reader who has followed the general train of thought of this book so far will no doubt have found yet another range of questions prompted by this chapter. You will have noticed that we have talked about tackling new words only in terms of the overt oral responses that the learner makes to them. How much does this matter? you may ask. What has it to do with "reading properly so called", the derivation of semantic meaning from print? Are not these 'errors' in pronunciation an integral part of that by-passing of the auditory level of perception that contributes to faster reading? Is it not a fact that a child may be able to read and comprehend words like *allege* and *copious* and *pique* without being sure how to say them? Indeed, would not most adults have to admit that there are some words which they understand when they read them in a book or a newspaper but which they hesitate to use in conversation for fear of mispronouncing them? True. But one mark of the literate adult is that he is always trying to narrow the gap between his passive and his active vocabularies, and that he *wants* to try out these partly-familiar words for his own purposes. All the more does a young learner need to make new words his own, and, even more than an adult, he needs a basis of confidence on which to do so. As we said earlier, to be able to utter a word is to have a further measure of control over it, to be able to use it, and to have an auditory as well as a visual image of it when you try to write it. What we have begun to investigate in this chapter is the kind of difficulty that a learner-reader of CES may encounter, so that his teachers can more systematically help him towards a greater confidence in *using* words. This means, among other things, ascertaining more accurately than we do now the point at which he can dispense with the scaffolding provided at the early stages by a phonemic teaching medium and later by graded teaching material using words that can be learnt by regular analogy.

There are two other related points to add. One is that 'Irregulars' as defined in this chapter are likely to produce in the highest degree the effects associated with the several inconsistencies of CES, since they may frustrate any of four perceptual processes. This means that they have the strongest tendency to condition the perception of words as wholes. It also means that the auditory level of perception is of the least help in providing a stepping stone to the semantic meaning. That is to say, it is possible for the teacher to associate a graphemic sequence like *stanchion* or *gunwale* directly with the semantic meaning without the intervention of clear auditory percepts; and it is equally possible to associate the corresponding phonemic sequence with the semantic meaning without a clear visual percept of the word. There is a three-way relationship, most closely analogous to that in a pure ideography, in which it is the semantic meaning that facilitates the association of the visual and auditory percepts. The reading of such words, in the proper sense, therefore requires the context of the larger Gestalten provided by sentence, paragraph, story or real-life experience. The ninety words in the test material can be read, in one sense, by a kind of barking at print; in another and better sense, they can be read only in the context of a tale (which we invite readers to compose) of how in the nineteenth century two gentlemen left their English gardens and sailed away to lands of spices and strange animals, of ceremonial mourning and uninhibited laughter.

8

Experiments with print

This chapter describes a group of three more complex but still relatively short investigations designed to test some of the main hypotheses that have been put forward on theoretical grounds earlier in this book. It is necessary to describe all the experiments in some detail before summarising the findings, because several variables were involved in each of them, and it will be seen that the whole of the field-work is inter-connected. The statistical part of the evidence is given with some visual representations of the results. The main findings are brought together for discussion in the final chapter.

In the theoretical analysis of perceptual processes in learning to read, we tried to bring out the following points. (1) There is a wide range of reading skills that may be at least as susceptible to the influence of various writing systems as to that of teaching methods. (2) These skills seem to be highly interdependent in their functioning and development. (3) While a fairly phonemic writing system appears to be most suitable for the formation of some basic reading skills, a phonemically unreliable system may be more conducive to the development of skills needed to achieve a higher rate of comprehension in reading than in listening. We suggested that some of these influences, despite their multiple interactions, might be to a certain extent measurable. Though it would be hopeless to aim at establishing exactly the nature and results of their interaction, yet study of any one influence in isolation would be both difficult and of little practical value. The experimental work described here is an attempt at compromise between these two extremes.

Tests and materials

Four writing systems were used: (a) *CES*, the conventional English spelling or traditional orthography; (b) *IPA*, the notation adopted by the International Phonetic Association; (c) *i.t.a.*, the 'Augmented

Roman' alphabet devised by Sir James Pitman for initial teaching purposes; and (d) *P.Sh.*, the more phonemic variety of the shorthand invented by Sir Isaac Pitman. Three separate experiments were made, and the following classes of subjects took part in one or more of them. *Class I* consisted of children who were in their first three years of learning to read, by whatever medium or method. *Class II* comprised children who were in the fourth, fifth or sixth year of learning to read; all the reading skills of this class of children were investigated while they were reading CES, whether they had been initially taught by means of this or of i.t.a. *Class III* included various groups of advanced readers at high school and college level. Each of the subjects in this class, whether foreign or a native speaker of English, was familiar with CES and with one form of phonemic notation, either IPA or P.Sh. Six tests were devised, each to test one of the following factors:

Test i: 'Graded Reading Vocabulary';
Test ii: 'translation' of unfamiliar 'Regular' and 'Irregular' spellings;
Test iii: perception of phrases under different conditions;
Test iv: help of phonemes to the short-term visual memory;
Test v: word-finding on pages of print;
Test vi: power and rate of comprehension in reading selected sentences and paragraphs from print in different writing systems.

In the following pages we describe in more detail the specific purpose of each test, and the instruments used, and then say how the tests were carried out.

Test i. 'Graded Reading Vocabulary'

As is well known, this is a test of the ability to 'recognise', in terms of speech-sounds, certain words which are at various levels of difficulty for a young learner. The instrument used for this test was also required to provide data about two more specific matters: (a) the facility in this recognition afforded by a phonemic writing system, and (b) the influence that this facility at the early stages of learning to read might have upon the development of reading vocabulary in a conventional writing system. These sets of data were obtained by the use of Schonell's R1 test in two versions: the original (i.e. in CES), and the i.t.a. version prepared by the Reading Research Unit of the London University Institute of Education.

Test ii. 'Translation' of unfamiliar 'Regular' and 'Irregular' spellings

This test was to establish what help is given by a phonemic system in 'translating' the two distinct categories of words in CES, 'Regulars' and 'Irregulars' being defined as previously explained in Chapter 7. A selected group of forty of the words used in the earlier investigation (see Table A at p. 97 above) was arranged in two lists, each containing 10 R's and 10 IR's. The words with f_m from 23 to 7 appeared to represent the same degree of familiarity to subjects in Class I as did those with f_m from 6 to 0·2 for subjects in Class II. Ten R's and ten IR's of higher f_m were separately written out in large letters both in CES and in i.t.a. It must be remembered that a word that is 'irregular' in CES will show less 'irregularity' when it is written in i.t.a.

Test iii. Perception of phrases under different conditions

The aim of this test was to investigate the hypothesis that a two-stage procedure for the teaching of reading, in which a phonemic notation is used before CES, promotes the growth of the visual 'field' in the average child. Here, because of some practical limitations, the visual field had to be measured in terms of the amount of visual information perceived and translated into the spoken counterparts in a given unit of time. The equipment largely consisted of specially-improvised mechanical devices, including a tape-recorder adapted to allow the tape to run outside the body of the machine in such a way that, with the recorder running at a controlled speed, words attached to the tape appeared in the same sequence as when a reader moves his eyes from left to right. A viewing box was designed to restrict the visibility of the tape to a pre-determined length of $3\frac{3}{4}$ inches, to keep a constant distance of 15 inches between the reader's eye and the tape, and to screen the body of the machine and other objects that might distract the reader. The linguistic material was selected from 'Neale Analysis' (1958) in CES and in the i.t.a. version. Three texts of graded degrees of difficulty were each divided into four sets of phrases (i.e. groups of words separated by oblique lines). The phrases were copied in the original letter sizes and styles on to white paper, and attached to the tape in serial order, with the spaces between phrases gradually decreasing in length. Thus, after the first set of phrases in each version there was a space equal to eleven times the length of the print; after the second set a space ten times the length of the print, and so on, so that no extra distance was left between the phrases of the twelfth set. Thus it was possible to assess (at least comparatively) the reader's span of recognition when he was asked to read the phrases aloud with the tape running at a controlled speed; the sooner a child stopped reading the phrases, the smaller was his recognition span. To read the first set of printed phrases at the lower speed of the tape, it was necessary theoretically to 'see' only half a letter per eye-fixation; to read the twelfth set at the higher speed, it was necessary to recognise two six-letter words per eye-fixation. It was assumed that any child of Classes I or II would possess a maximum span somewhere between these two extremes. This method of testing does not of course measure skills at the purely visual level. Inevitably, at the very high speeds (the maximum required the pronunciation of 450 words per minute) there would be errors due to sheer difficulty of articulation. Besides, since the spaces occur after phrases and not after smaller units of print, the span of recognition is not directly proportionate to the serial number of the set reached. However, the test does provide a basis for comparisons of results.

Test iv. Help of phonemes to the short-term visual memory

A crucial part of the experimental work was to test the hypothesis that, when the span of recognition is smaller than a morpheme, the reader tends to 'translate' his visual percepts into some auditory counterparts, in order to clear the short-term visual memory before the next fixation. A corollary of this is that it is easier to reproduce a sequence of shapes that are associated with simple auditory percepts (such as the letters of an alphabet) than to reproduce a similar sequence of characters, simpler in shape, but not having any comparable auditory counterparts. For this test, certain letters were selected so as to fulfil the following conditions: (a) that they are used in both CES and i.t.a.; (b) that they could be used for the composition of a sufficient number of nonsense-syllables or words; and (c) that they are made up of reasonably simple shapes. The letters *a*, *e* and *o* were selected as associates of vowels, and the letters *b*, *d* and *k* as associates of consonants. The following characters made o simple shapes were used: a circle, a square and a triangle to match *a*, *e* and *o* respectively, and the same geometrical figures with an added vertical stroke at the base of each to match *b*, *d* and *k* respectively. The six letters were combined so as to represent eight pronounceable nonsense words of varying length, and then corresponding characters were used in similar groups. For example, the letter-sequence *a d e k o* was matched by the character-sequence:

$$\bigcirc \ \text{Ḅ} \ \square \ \text{Ą} \ \triangle$$

Purely at the visual level there would appear to be no significant difference between the two sequences in the ease with which their shapes can be discriminated or can be stored in the short-term visual memory. On theoretical grounds, however, it was expected that children would commit more errors in copying the character-sequences that had no auditory counterparts. The six letters, the six characters and eight sequences of each kind were copied on to separate cards. The viewing box used in Test ii was adapted for tachistoscopic exposures, mainly by the addition of a hinged flap which served for storing the cards in the required order, for exposing them at a definite point in space to which children could easily re-orientate their attention after each 'copying', and for allowing simultaneous manipulation of tachistoscope and chronometer.

In order to suggest to the testees that the test consisted mainly of 'copying', and to reduce the tendency to use auditory percepts as an aid, the set of fourteen cards containing 'simple shapes' was exposed

Figure 9: Recording sheet for Test iv

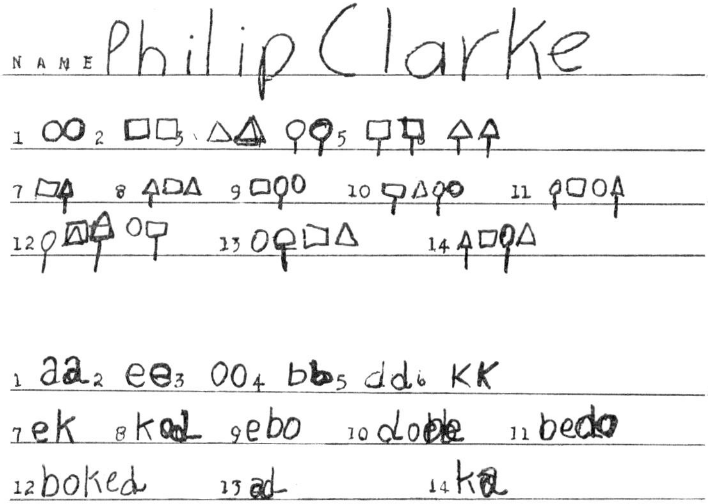

first. The exposure time of each card, in both sets, was three seconds; the interval between exposures of course varied, because it had to last until every child in a group had stopped 'copying' from memory. A recording sheet is illustrated in Figure 9. The six cards bearing individual characters were exposed first, to ensure that the procedure was understood. The children were then told that in the next part of the game, more shapes would appear on each single card, and had to be copied on the sheet of paper. Similar instructions were given before the exposure of the cards bearing letter-shapes, great care being taken to avoid the use of the word 'letter'.

Test v. Word-finding on pages of print

The purpose of this test was to provide data for assessing the influence of different teaching media upon the ability to store images of whole words for a considerable period of time, for instance whilst reading a long sentence or a paragraph. This required the use of texts well standardised and graded with respect to level of familiarity with print; Form C of 'Neale Analysis' was selected for this purpose, and was used in the CES and i.t.a. versions. One word was selected from each right-hand page of this form, words from the first three pages being used for subjects in Class I, and words from the last three pages for subjects in Class II. The words were so selected as (a) to be sufficiently far from the beginning of the page, so that the subject had to store the image of a particular word for a period of time; (b) to appear in different areas of print and thus discourage the subject from looking first at the point where he found the word on the preceding page; (c) to be at corresponding levels of familiarity to the two groups of subjects; and (d) to be only rarely employed on the page in question. Form C of 'Neale Analysis' was prepared in the following ways: each selected word was copied in the same style and size below the picture on the left-hand page; a paper flap was attached on each right-hand page so as to keep the print covered until the subject was required to start searching for the word; and tabs of gradually reduced length were attached to the bottom right-hand corner of each page used in the test, so as to facilitate turning the pages. Form B of 'Neale Analysis' was prepared in the same way, and used for practice tests to ensure that the instructions were fully understood. In the actual test the child had first to read aloud the word beneath the picture, which was the signal for the tester to uncover the printed page, and then the child had to point with his finger to the same word as soon as he found it among the print. The test yielded two variables: (i) the time of finding three words on three printed pages (the reciprocal value of which time gives the relative speed of different subjects in finding particular items in different contexts), and (ii) the number of correctly pronounced words in certain texts, which corresponds with certain levels of literacy. Of particular importance was the correlation of these two variables, and the comparison between these correlations in the reading of two different writing systems. For example, a higher correlation in the results from testing in the CES version than in the i.t.a. version would indicate that the skill to 'recognise' words in terms of sound is linked with the 'higher' skills more closely in reading a conventional orthography than in reading a more phonemic notation. This would suggest that, whereas the 'translation' of visual into auditory percepts might be important for the development of reading vocabulary, it provides no reliable symptoms of the state of any other skills; or, to put it another way, the final benefits of a teaching medium that facilitates such 'translation' could be measured only after the transfer to conventional orthography.

Test vi. Power and rate of comprehension in reading selected sentences and paragraphs from print in different writing systems

Since the principal goal of reading is the understanding of printed messages, it is important to study the influence of writing systems upon the development of the power of comprehension, with particular reference to texts of different levels of difficulty for certain classes of subjects. This requires the differentiation of the various components of reading efficiency, and the correlation of these components with other data such as chronological age and verbal intelligence at the date of school entry. Test vi therefore was designed to provide, in conjunction with Tests i–v, some data for assessing the effects of different media at different stages of reading ability, and the degree to which separate skills participate in the power of comprehension and also in the rate of comprehending texts of different levels of difficulty. The data were obtained by using the first and second parts of a graded comprehension test (written in various systems), taking into account the time taken to complete each of them. The material had to be suitable—at least to some extent—for subjects in Classes I and II and for some in Class III; while the first part had to permit an average child in Class I to achieve about 50% of the maximum score, the second part had to be such that no child in Class II could achieve significantly more, whatever the writing system used. The material also had to allow the measurement of finer differences, i.e. differences between groups of subjects of the same class but taught by different media, and differences within the same group when the subjects use different writing systems. There were two groups of material in this test, which were used as follows.

1 *Comprehension of Individual Sentences*   On the basis of a pilot test, the material used in A. F. Watts' (1958) 'Sentence Reading Test I' was divided into two, Part One containing sentences 1-7 and Part Two containing sentences 18-35. Then the original material was transcribed also into i.t.a. and P.Sh. The i.t.a. version was administered to children who had been taught by this medium and had not yet transferred to CES. The corresponding CES version was used with other children of Classes I and II. The P.Sh. version, together with the CES version, was administered to those subjects in Class III who possessed a high degree of competence in reading and writing shorthand (Pitman's). It was necessary to make a few modifications of the procedure described in Watts' Manual. With Class III, all the subjects present were divided into two sub-groups X and Y with equal number of subjects and as far as possible the same sex-distribution. Part One of the CES version was given to sub-group X and Part One of the P.Sh. version to sub-group Y. The sub-groups started the tests simultaneously, and as soon as any subject from either sub-group gave the signal that he or she had completed the test, all the others had to stop work. Then Part Two of the CES version was given to sub-group Y and Part Two of the P.Sh. version to sub-group X, the timing of the test being determined in the same way.

2 *Comprehension of Paragraphs*   The original (CES) paragraphs of N.F.E.R. (1958) Test 2, Comprehension, were transcribed also in IPA. Both CES and IPA versions were then divided into two parts, the first containing paragraphs 1-3 and the second containing paragraphs 4-6. The test was administered to Class III subjects at College of Education level who were familiar with IPA. The procedure was as described above for Class III subjects, and the instruction in the test manual modified accordingly.

Using this battery of six tests, an investigation was carried out in three stages which we now describe, with some analysis of the findings at each stage.

Subjects and results

Three separate but related experiments were organised. The scope of each was determined by two main considerations: (a) the level of literacy of the prospective subjects (Classes I and II were sufficiently close in age for some common experimentation, but Classes II and III mostly were not), and (b) the possible interactions of different teaching procedures with the influence of different writing systems. These considerations apply to the three experiments as follows.

Experiment I: (a) low level of literacy
                 (b) variety of teaching methods
Experiment II: (a) low level of literacy (as in Exper. I)
                 (b) variety of teaching media
Experiment III: (a) high level of literacy
                 (b) variety of writing systems in use

Experiment I

The purposes of this experiment required that the subjects be of about the same chronological age as the subjects for Experiment II (i.e. in Class I, 6–7 years old, and in Class II, 9–10 years old), and that in each of these two classes there were groups of subjects who had been taught to read by different methods but who were matched in every other respect. The programme was carried out in two London schools, each of whom initially provided 25 subjects in Class I and another 25 in Class II. School 'A' laid a strong emphasis on teaching to read by using 'phonics', and School 'B' laid no particular emphasis on any one teaching method. For the purposes of this enquiry, the groups provided by School 'A' can be considered as 'Phonics' and those provided by School 'B' as 'Look-Say', as long as we remember that the differences between the performances of the groups indicate the nature, but not the extent, of the influence of these two teaching methods.

Owing to the length of the experiment, not all the children initially provided by School 'B' were able to participate in all of the tests of the pilot battery listed below, and thus the number in each 'Look-Say' group was reduced to 20. Since those excluded from these groups were mostly children with a relatively low Reading Age as measured by Test i, the matching of the groups for the purposes of analysing the results was made by ignoring the scores of five children in each 'Phonic' group who had low achievements on Test i. The relevant data on the four final groups of children is shown in Table E.

Table E: Final groups of subjects in Experiment I

GROUPS	Chronological Age		Number of Subjects		
	Range	Average	Boys	Girls	Total
Class I 'Phonics'	7.0–7.7	7.3	10	10	20
'Look-Say'	6.8–7.5	7.1	8	12	20
Class II 'Phonics'	9.1–9.7	9.3	9	11	20
'Look-Say'	9.0–9.9	9.4	9	11	20

Incidentally, the administration of the pilot-battery of tests in this experiment led to some useful modifications of material and procedures for Experiment II. But principally the tests were administered in such a way as to measure eight different variables, in the following sequence.

Using Test i:
    (1) RA: Reading Age.
Using Test v:
    (2) TFW: time taken to find specific words on printed pages, the reciprocal value of which is the speed of finding words (SFW); and
    (3) ProW: pronunciation of these specific words.
Using Test iii:
    (4) EPh: speed of perceiving easy phrases; and
    (5) DPh: speed of perceiving difficult phrases.
Using Test ii:
    (6) R's: 'translation' of 'Regulars', and
    (7) IR's   'translation' of 'Irregulars'.
Using Test vi:
    (8) PC: power of comprehension.

The use of these abbreviations may at first sight appear rather forbidding and tiresome, but in fact you will probably find them quite easy to follow, and they will be useful in presenting the results of the investigation. The main data concerning the four groups of children are, presented in three different ways, in Table F, Figure 10 and Table G.

Table F gives in the first four columns the arithmetical mean and the standard deviation for each group in respect of the eight

Table F: Main data from Experiment I

VARIABLE	CLASS II		CLASS I		Level of statistical significance in differences between :		
	Phonics	L–S	Phonics	L–S	Cl.	T.M.	Int.[1]
1. R.A. Mean	11.4	10.1	8.7	6.6	1%	1%	—
S.D.	1.2	2.0	1.2	1.0			
2. TFW Mean	63.0	69.5	50.0	119.0	—	1%	5%
S.D.	20.0	24.8	25.6	56.4			
3. ProW Mean	2.6	2.5	2.6	1.9	—	5%	—
S.D.	0.5	0.8	0.8	0.9			
4. EPh Mean	7.8	6.4	3.0	2.3	1%	5%	—
S.D.	0.9	2.2	1.5	1.9			
5. DPh Mean'	6.3	5.4	4.8	1.7	1%	5%	—
S.D.	2.9	4.0	2.9	2.8			
6. 'R's' Mean	9.2	7.7	6.7	2.0	1%	1%	1%
S.D.	0.7	2.6	2.2	3.0			
7. 'IR's' Mean	2.3	1.5	2.1	0.7	—	1%	—
S.D.	1.3	1.6	1.3	1.2			
8. PC Mean	22.6	23.8	15.4	5.1	1%	5%	1%
S.D.	7.6	8.4	6.1	5.3			

1) The following abbreviations stand for : Cl. − Classes; T.M. − Teaching Methods; Int. − Interaction.

variables. The next three columns show the level of statistical significance of the differences between groups, first in comparing Classes, secondly in comparing teaching methods, and finally in the interaction between the two. The data concerning variance estimates were worked out by the University of London Computer Unit.

Figure 10: Relative achievements of groups in Classes I and II initially taught by different teaching methods

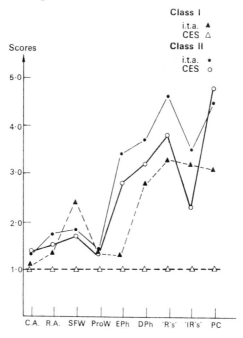

The data in the first four columns of Table F are shown in another way in Figure 10, where the relative achievements of the groups are represented in terms of 'profiles'. The abbreviations on the base line stand for chronological age and for the eight variables measured in the tests. The average chronological age and the mean scores on each test of the 'Look-Say' group in Class I are taken as the unit of the ordinate, represented by the horizontal broken line. The data for the other groups are shown in relation to this unit.

The most interesting feature of the 'profiles' (Figure 10) concerns the power of comprehension: although groups of 'Phonics' are superior on all the other variables, the Class II group of 'Look-

Say' children are ahead of them in PC—despite a remarkable lead that 'Phonics' show in this respect at a younger age. The most noticeable superiority of 'Phonics' in both classes is in 'translation' of unfamiliar spellings, both 'Regular' and 'Irregular'; this agrees with the results of the previous investigation described in Chapter 7.

Table G: Coefficients of correlation between 8 variables

	1 R.A.	2 TFW	3 ProW	4 EPh	5 DPh	6 R's	7 IR's	8 PC
1 R.A.		.8/-.7	.8/ .7	.7/ .7	.8/ .8	.7/ .9	.6/ .9	.7/ .9
2 TFW	-.1/-.7		-.9/-.9	-.7/-.6	-.7/-.6	-.6/-.6	-.8/-.5	-.6/-.5
3 ProW	.5/ .7	-.4/-.9		.7/ .5	.8/ .6	.6/ .5	.8/ .5	.6/ .5
4 EPh	.3/ .7	.2/-.6	.3/ .5		.8/ .5	.8/ .5	.7/ .4	.8/ .5
5 DPh	.7/ .9	.2/-.6	.4/ .6	.5/ .5		.7/ .8	.6/ .8	.8/ 8
6 R's	.3/ .9	.0/-.6	.0/ .5	.0/ .5	.4/ .8		.7/ .9	.7/ .8
7 IR's	.4/ .9	-.2/-.5	.3/ .5	.0/ .4	.3/ .8	.3/ .9		.6/ .8
8 PC	.6/ .9	.2/-.5	.4/ .5	.2/ .5	.5/ .8	.3/ .8	.1/ .8	

Another way of comparing the results will bring out more specifically the interdependence of various reading skills. The coefficients of correlation between the eight variables have been computed separately for each of the four groups of children. They are shown, rounded to the first decimal figure, in Table G. The upper triangle in the table relates to Class I, and the lower triangle to Class II; the figure to the left of the stroke refers to 'Phonics' and the figure to the right refers to 'Look-Say'. To make full use of this table, it is necessary to know the level of statistical significance of each coefficient of correlation (on the basis of $N = 20$, for 5% level $r > 0.423$ and for 1% level $r > 0.575$), and also the relationship of the corresponding coefficients for different groups of subjects. For example, the coefficient of correlation between R.A. and DPh is significant at 1% level for 'Phonics' and 'Look-Say' in Class II; but a comparison of the actual r-values (0.7 and 0.9 respectively) would indicate that the interdependence of the skills involved in the variables is significantly higher with the 'Look-Say' group of children. Again, the relatively low achievement in comprehension

of 'Phonics' in Class II, despite their marked superiority in 'translating' both 'Regulars' and 'Irregulars', is compatible with the relatively low level of correlation between PC, R's and IR's in this
group as compared with the 'Look-Say' group in the same Class.

In general, the figures support the view that 'mechanical' skills in
reading are no guarantee for comprehension in silent reading. For a
moderately advanced learner initially taught with some emphasis on
'Phonics', power of comprehension varies mainly with R.A. and with
DPh, which in turn varies significantly with EPh—i.e. with perception of phrases, both easy and difficult—but not with the 'lower'
skills. For other groups of children—younger 'Phonics' and both
'Look-Say' groups—comprehension is related to all the other variables on the list.

So much for the Experiment I, which not only served as a pilot
for the rest of the programme but also provided some of the evidence
that is discussed in Chapter 9.

Experiment II

The purpose of this experiment was to measure some of the factors
which interact with the influence of writing systems in the development of reading skills. It required matched groups of subjects who
had started learning to read by different media. Four pairs of schools
in Walsall (Staffs.) and Oldham (Lancs.) provided four groups of 40
children—two groups for Class I testing, and two for Class II. In
each class one group had been initially taught to read by i.t.a. and
then transferred to CES, while the other had been taught by means
of CES throughout. The Class I children had been given no I.Q.
test before they started learning to read; the matching of the two
groups in this class was as shown in Table H. All the Class II
children had been given the Crichton Intelligence Test immediately
before starting learning to read in September 1961; their matching
was as shown in Table I. The schools which provided these children
are designated by initial letters beneath the abbreviations for the
teaching media. In view of the usual field difficulties (distance between schools, absence due to illness), the tests were carried out with
a larger number of children than is shown in the Tables, and the final
matching of groups was done only after the testing programme had
been completed. To qualify for the inclusion in a group of final matching, every subject had to have participated in the whole programme,
so that the data could be correlated as described under Experiment I.

This time the experiment dealt with thirteen basic variables,

Table H: Matching of children in Class I

SCHOOL ENTRY DATE	CHILDREN	SCHOOLS [1)				TOTAL	
		CES		i.t.a.		CLASS I	
		E.A.	D.R.	B.B.	D.B.	CES	i.t.a.
Jan. 1964	Number	10		10		10	10
	Boys	3		2		3	2
	Girls	7		8		7	8
	Av. Age	7.27		7.25		7.27	7.25
April 1964	Number	5		5		5	5
	Boys	1		2		1	2
	Girls	4		3		4	3
	Av. Age	6.87		6.97		6.87	6.97
Sept. 1964	Number	5	8	5	8	13	13
	Boys	2	3	1	5	5	6
	Girls	3	5	4	3	8	7
	Av. Age	6.67	6.64	6.57	6.57	6.65	6.57
Jan. 1965	Number		7		7	7	7
	Boys		1		3	1	3
	Girls		6		4	6	4
	Av. Age		6.30		6.29	6.30	6.29
April 1965	Number		5		5	5	5
	Boys		1		1	1	1
	Girls		4		4	4	4
	Av. Age		6.03		5.97	6.03	5.97
SUM TOTAL	NUMBER	20	20	20	20	40	40
	BOYS	6	5	5	9	11	14
	GIRLS	14	15	15	11	29	26
	AV. AGE	7.0	6.4	7.0	6.4	6.7	6.7

1) The Infants' Schools which provided these children are shown in the table by the Head-teachers' initials beneath the usual abbreviations for the teaching media.

Table I: Matching of children in Class II

CHILDREN		SCHOOLS				TOTAL	
		CES		i.t.a.		CLASS II	
		St.H.	Lim.	St.M.	F.H.	CES	i.t.a.
BOYS		11	9	13	7	20	20
GIRLS		9	11	7	13	20	20
Crichton Raw Scores	7–10	4	2	1	5	6	6
	11–15	7	7	5	10	14	15
	16–20	6	5	9	5	11	14
	21–25	3	5	4	–	8	4
	26–30	–	1	1	–	1	1
Socio-Economic Classes	2	–	–	–	1	–	1
	3	12	16	6	12	28	18
	4	6	4	11	6	10	17
	5	2	–	3	1	2	4
Age Range	8:6 – 8:8	3	3	3	11	6	14
	8:9 – 8:11	7	4	4	7	11	11
	9:0 – 9:2	6	4	10	1	10	11
	9:3 – 9:5	4	9	3	1	13	4
Average Age		9.0	9.2	9.0	8.9	9.10	8.95

listed below in the sequence of their collection, with the method used shown in brackets.

(1) Cr./CA: for Class II, the I.Q. as measured by the Crichton Intelligence Test; for Class I, the chronological age.

(2) RC1: rate of comprehension of relatively simple sentences (the first part of Test vi-1).

(3) RC2: rate of comprehension of relatively difficult sentences (the second part of Test vi-1).

(4) PC: power of comprehension (the total score on Test vi within a common time limit).

(5) R.A.: reading age (Test i).

(6) R's: 'translation' of 'Regulars' (Test ii).

(7) IR's: 'translation' of 'Irregulars' (Test ii).

(8) PhHS: perception of phrases at higher speed (Test iii).

(9) PhLS: perception of phrases at lower speed (Test iii)

(10) MSSS: short-term memory for sequences of simple shapes (Test iv).

(11) MNS: short-term memory for nonsense syllables (Test iv).

(12) TFW: time taken to find specific words on printed pages, the reciprocal value being the speed (SFW) (Test v).

(13) ProW: pronunciation of the above words (Test v).

Individual raw scores were arranged as follows: for children in Class II, rank-ordered according to scores on the Cr. test on the date of school entry; for children in Class I, grouped according to the number of terms they had had at school.

The data are here presented in three ways, as for Experiment I. Table J gives the arithmetical means of scores, standard deviations, and levels of significance of differences between levels of literacy and between teaching media. Relative achievements are shown as 'profiles' in Figure 11, where the unit of the ordinate represents the average age and the mean score on each test of the CES children in Class I. Three points are worthy of special note. (a) The younger i.t.a. group scored lowest in tests of comprehension, except for a slight superiority over other children of the same age in PC. (b) The younger i.t.a. group scored significantly higher than any other group in 'translating' unfamiliar 'Irregulars'. (c) The older i.t.a. group scored higher than CES children on every single test in the battery.

Table J: Main data from Experiment II

VARIABLE		CLASS II		CLASS I		Level of statistical significance in differences between		
		i.t.a.	CES	i.t.a.	CES	Cl.	Med.	Int.[1]
2. RC1	Mean	6.1	3.3	0.8	0.94	1%	1%	1%
	S.D.	3.8	2.2	0.7	1.0			
3. RC2	Mean	1.5	0.87	0.2	0.22	1%	1%	1%
	S.D.	0.6	0.5	0.3	0.4			
4. PC	Mean	26.0	21.2	8.92	8.8	1%	5%	—
	S.D.	5.6	8.0	5.6	6.5			
5. R.A.	Mean	10.8	9.5	8.0	7.3	1%	1%	—
	S.D.	1.5	1.8	1.1	1.1			
6. "R's"	Mean	9.2	7.5	6.8	5.2	1%	1%	—
	S.D.	2.0	3.4	2.6	3.0			
7. "IR's"	Mean	1.3	0.7	5.9	1.3	1%	1%	—
	S.D.	1.2	0.9	2.5	1.4			
8. PhHS	Mean	8.1	6.6	4.3	3.1	1%	1%	—
	S.D.	1.5	2.6	2.4	2.2			
9. PhLS	Mean	10.4	8.7	5.9	4.4	1%	1%	—
	S.D.	1.5	2.9	2.3	2.2			
10. MSSS	Mean	3.4	3.3	1.1	1.0	1%	—	—
	S.D.	1.3	1.5	1.1	1.0			
11. MNS	Mean	7.4	6.6	4.3	4.5	1%	—	—
	S.D.	0.9	1.6	2.1	1.7			
12. TFW	Mean	60.0	86.7	75.2	85.5	—	1%	—
	S.D.	21.0	47.0	23.6	55.0			
13. ProW	Mean	2.7	2.2	2.8	2.4	—	1%	—
	S.D.	0.6	0.8	0.4	0.7			

1) The following abbreviations stand for : Cl. — Classes; Med. — Teaching Media; Int. — Interaction.

The interdependence of various reading skills under the influence of different teaching media can be studied in Table K, using the same technique as described under Experiment I. Correlation coefficients between all the thirteen variables have been computed for each of the four groups separately; rounded to the first decimal place, they are set out in two parallelograms, the first relating to i.t.a. and the second to CES groups, and the upper and lower triangles

Figure 11: Relative achievements of groups in Classes I and II initially taught by different teaching media

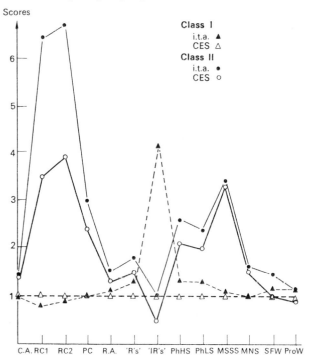

relating to Classes I and II respectively. It will be seen that in both groups and whichever initial teaching medium was used, Reading Age is significantly correlated with comprehension (RC1, RC2 and PC) and also with 'translation' of 'Regulars' and 'Irregulars'. Again, irrespective of teaching media, scores on perception of phrases (variables 8 and 9) are correlated highly with speed of finding words and pronunciation of words (variables 12 and 13), but not with short-term memory for sequences of simple shapes (variable 10).

Table K: Coefficients of correlation between 13 variables

i.t.a.

	1	2	3	4	5	6	7	8	9	10	11	12	13
1 Cr.		5	.5	.5	.4	.3	.2	.6	.6	.2	.4	.3	.3
2 RC1	.1		.7	.9	.6	.5	.4	.6	.5	.2	.6	.5	.3
3 RC2	.4	.1		.7	.5	.4	.2	.5	.5	.3	.4	.4	.2
4 PC	.4	.3	.6		.7	.6	.5	.7	.6	.2	.7	.5	.4
5 R.A.	.4	.5	.5	.8		.7	.6	.7	.5	.2	.6	.6	.4
6 'R's'	.3	.3	.3	.8	.7		.8	.6	.7	.0	.7	.6	.5
7 'IR's'	.3	.2	.1	.4	.5	.4		.5	.5	.0	.6	.4	.4
8 PhHS	.5	.2	.5	.8	.7	.7	.4		.7	.2	.7	.5	.5
9 PhLS	.3	.4	.4	.7	.7	.7	.4	.6		-.1	.5	.6	.5
10 MSSS	.0	.0	-.1	-.1	.0	-.3	-.1	.1	-.1		.3	.0	.1
11 MNS	-.1	.0	.3	.3	.4	.5	.3	.4	.3	-.1		.3	.5,
12 TFW	.4	.4	.4	.8	.8	.8	.3	.7	.6	-.2	.4		.4
13 ProW	.1	.3	.4	.7	.7	.8	.4	.7	.6	.0	.5	.7	

CES

	1	2	3	4	5	6	7	8	9	10	11	12	13
1 Cr.		.5	.2	.6	.5	.3	.3	.5	.5	-.2	.1	.6	.6
2 RCl	.4		.5	.8	.6	.6	.6	.8	.8	.0	.1	.6	.5
3 RC2	.5	.7		.7	.5	.4	.5	.4	.6	.3	.2	.4	.4
4 PC	.4	.8	.8		.8	.8	.6	.8	.9	.1	.3	.7	.7
5 R.A.	.4	.8	.7	.9		.8	.6	.8	.9	.1	.4	.7	.7
6 'R's'	.2	.7	.6	.8	.9		.6	.7	.8	.1	.3	.7	.7
7 'IR's'	.3	.5	.5	.6	.6	.4		.6	.6	.0	.1	.4	.6
8 PhHS	.3	.8	.7	.9	.9	.8	.5		.9	.0	.1	.7	.6
9 PhLS	.4	.8	.7	.8	.8	.7	.4	.8		.1	.3	.8	.7
10 MSSS	.1	.3	.1	.2	.2	.1	.1	.2	.1		.2	.0	.0
11 MNS	.2	.5	.4	.5	.6	.6	.3	.5	.4	.3		.4	.3
12 TFW	.3	.7	.6	.8	.8	.8	.4	.8	.6	.2	.5		.7
13 ProW	.4	.7	.6	.8	.8	.7	.5	.8	.7	.1	.4	-.8	

Indeed, with older i.t.a. children, there is a conspicuously low—and frequently negative—correlation between scores on MSSS and on tests concerning any other variable. On the other hand, if we look at the correlations between perception of phrases (variable 8) and short-term memory for nonsense syllables (variable 11) in Class I, we see a remarkable difference between the groups of children initially taught by the two different systems: for young CES children the correlation is low (below 20% level of significance), but for young i.t.a. children the correlation is high (far above the 1% level). In general, the pattern of correlation noticed in the pilot test emerges again, though somewhat modified. In this experiment the correlation between the variables concerning comprehension (2, 3 and 4) and those involved with mechanical skills (5–13) are actually somewhat lower for groups of children who showed particular proficiency in the latter group of skills. Thus, although the i.t.a. group in Class I scored highly on IR's, this achievement correlates with comprehension to a noticeably lesser degree than does the corresponding achievement of CES children in the same class. Similarly, although the i.t.a. group of Class II scored higher than the CES group on every single test, all the correlations between comprehension and the 'mechanical' variables are significantly lower for this group than for the matched CES group. In other words, the superior attainment of the older i.t.a. group in reading proper does not seem to be attributable solely to superiority in the 'mechanical' skills.

In order to assess the role played by a phonemic writing system (as represented by i.t.a.) in the formation of reading skills, we must look at the scores of certain matched sub-groups within the total age-range covered by the investigation. Let us first consider Class I, the sub-groups in this case being determined by the number of terms for which the children had attended school. 'Profiles' are shown in Figure 12.

The abbreviations on the base line stand for the same variables as in Figure 11 on p. 127. The unit of the ordinate—marked by the horizontal line—represents the average age and the mean score on each test of the CES children from School 'D.R.', where the children had had less than five terms' attendance. The relative achievements of children initially taught by i.t.a. are denoted by the black symbols, the triangle referring to children from School 'D.B.' (less than five terms' school attendance) and the circle referring to children from School 'B.B.' (average of more than five terms' attendance). The white symbols denote the relative achievements of the CES children from School 'E.A.' (average of more than five terms' attendance).

It can be seen that though the youngest group of i.t.a. children showed a remarkable superiority in the 'translation' of 'Irregulars' (which, you will remember, would appear less 'irregular' in i.t.a.), they scored less well in rate of comprehension. The sub-group with approximately two terms of further schooling had gained an advantage over the matched CES group in rate of comprehension of

Figure 12: Relative achievements of sub-groups in Class I

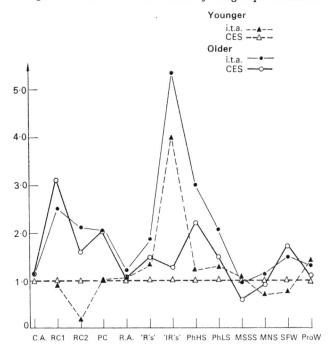

more difficult sentences (RC2), though not of easier ones, nor in speed of finding words on printed pages. But, as we have already seen (Table J, p. 126 and Figure 11, p. 127), two years after transfer to CES, the children initially taught by i.t.a. scored higher on every test.

It is also instructive to examine the performance of different sub-groups in Class II. In this case we can subdivide the Class according to their scores on the Crichton Intelligence Test on the date of school entry. Figure 13 shows that the gains of i.t.a. children in

Figure 13: Relative achievements of sub-groups in Class II

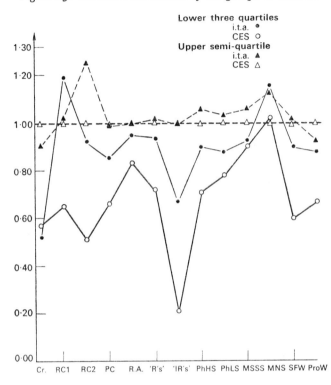

the lower three quartiles of the I.Q. list are even more obvious than those of the children of the highest ability.

In Figure 13 the abbreviations on the base line stand for the Crichton Intelligence Test (Cr.) and the twelve variables measured in the experiment. The unit of the ordinate (horizontal line and white triangle) represents the mean score on each test of the five CES children who scored highest on Cr. The relative achievements of the other CES children are marked with the white circle, those of the matched i.t.a. group with the black circle, and those of the five i.t.a. children with the highest Cr. scores by the black triangle.

This analysis certainly seems to indicate that a two-stage procedure in teaching to read—using a fairly phonemic writing system before CES—is of especial benefit to average children, representing perhaps three-quarters of all children in Junior Schools.

Finally, one detail of the results seems to bring out the importance of auditory percepts in comprehension of printed material at the

Junior-School level. In Watts' Sentence Comprehension Test I, the correct choice for the completion of Sentence 30 is the word 'reasonable', and one of the incorrect alternatives is 'excepted'. The choices made by Class II children were as follows:

	'reasonable'	'excepted'	Others	None	Total
i.t.a.	20	17	3	—	40
CES	7	6	15	12	40

The choice of 'excepted' by such a relatively large proportion of i.t.a. children, who scored highly on PC, is interesting, because a word very similar at the auditory level ('accepted') would have been a logically possible choice.

Experiment III

The purpose of this experiment was to secure some data about the influence of a semi-ideography such as CES upon adults' rates of comprehension in reading. For comparison, two forms of more phonemic writing systems were used: P.Sh. (Pitman's Shorthand or Stenography, though it is not completely phonemic) for comparison in reading sentences, and IPA (notation of the International Phonetic Association) for comparison in reading paragraphs, as described under Test vi above (p. 115). Subjects for the test with P.Sh. were highly fluent stenographers in the English language, who were provided by Pitman's College, London. The matching of groups of subjects is shown in Table L. A member of Group 'X' was the first to signal the completion of the easier part of the test,

Table L: Matching of groups for testing the rate of comprehension in reading CES and P.Sh.

GROUPS	Chronological Age		Number of Subjects		
	Range	Average	Male	Female	Total
Group 'X' : CES version 1–17 P.Sh. version 18–35	18–30	24.6	7	13	20
Group 'Y' : P.Sh. version 1–17 CES version 18–35	17–26	20.2	8	12	20

towards the end of the fourth minute after starting, and a member of Group 'Y' was the first to announce the completion of the more difficult part, towards the end of the eighth minute after starting that part.

The main data concerning the results are shown in Table M, and the raw scores of individual subjects have been rank-ordered for further analysis. The analysis of variance in the scores shows that while the difference between trials—i.e. reading the two different versions of the test—is significant at 1% level for both parts of the test, the interaction between the proficiency of the subjects and the two

Table M: Mean raw scores and analysis of variance testing CES and P.Sh.

DESCRIPTION	Sentences 1–17		Sentences 18–35		p-factor 1) for sentences	
	GROUPS					
	'X'	'Y'	'X'	'Y'	1–17	18–35
Mean Raw Score						
Subclass 'A'	17.0	13.4	17.4	13.2		
Subclass 'B'	16.5	6.9	14.8	8.0		
Variance Estimate						
Within Groups		4.0		5.7		
Between Groups		122.5		152.1	1%	1%
Between Trials		435.6		302.5	1%	1%
Interaction		90.0		16.9	1%	—

1) Level of statistical significance in the differences.

writing systems in reading more difficult sentences is even more highly significant.

In other words, the rate of comprehension varies significantly more with the systems of writing—being higher with CES—than with the subjects' proficiency in reading.

For testing CES in comparison with IPA the subjects were students of speech-therapy and phonetics at three different Colleges of London University. The matching of subjects is shown in Table N.

The raw scores were grouped according to the length of time that the subjects had had for intensive practice of reading IPA. Those who

Table N: Matching of groups for testing the rate of comprehension in reading CES and IPA

GROUPS	Chronological Age		Number of Subjects		
	Range	Average	Male	Female	Total
Group 'X' CES version 1–3 IPA version 4–6	18–41	26	18	17	35
Group 'Y' IPA version 1–3 CES version 4–6	18–38	25	16	19	35

Table O: Mean raw scores and analysis of variance testing CES and IPA

	Para. 1–3		Para. 4–6		p-factor [1) for para.	
	G R O U P S					
	'X'	'Y'	'X'	'Y'	1–3	4–6
Mean Raw Score						
Subclass 'A'	10.9	6.3	10.0	4.25		
Subclass 'B'	6.7	3.53	9.9	3.4		
Standard deviation	4.2	2.7	3.4	3.3		
Variance Estimate						
Within 'A' & 'B'	13.5		15.1			
Between 'A' & 'B'	207.0		3.6		1%	—
Between 'X' & 'Y'	280.0		648.1		1%	1%
Interaction	9.9		2.6		—	—

1) Level of statistical significance in the differences.

had had more than one year of such practice are referred to in the following analysis as Sub-class 'A', and those with less than one years' practice as Sub-class 'B'. Despite this difference between the sub-classes, in each test a member of Group 'X' was always the first to complete the test on paragraphs 1–3, and a member of Group 'Y' was always the first to complete the test on paragraphs 4–6, the announcement of completion on each occasion coming towards the end of the fifth minute of the part of the test concerned. The equal duration of testing time for all groups made it possible to produce the analysis of variance on the basis of raw scores; the main data are given in Table O.

The correlation between the scores of each group of subjects is significant at the 1% level, the coefficient of correlation between scores of Group 'X' being 0·575 and that of Group 'Y' 0·680. This suggests the importance of a 'general factor' in reading ability: the rate of comprehension achieved in one system of writing will, to a considerable extent, be transferred when the system of writing is changed. Another important feature of the analysis is that the difference between the Sub-classes 'A' and 'B' in their rate of comprehension is below the 5% level of statistical significance, i.e. after the further year of training the difference between performance in the two systems was virtually unaltered. On the other hand, the difference between the achievements of the two Groups 'X' and 'Y' is significant at 1% level for both parts of the test. In other words, in whatever order the different versions of the test were presented, both groups achieved a better comprehension rate in reading CES than in reading IPA.

9
Some inferences

The findings in the investigation we have described seem to bear out the theoretical propositions made in earlier chapters, in the following ways.

1) Average children of Class I (i.e. in the first three years of learning to read) who have been taught i.t.a. before CES score higher on all 'mechanical' skills, and average children of Class II (i.e. in the fourth, fifth and sixth years of learning to read) who were similarly taught score better in both 'mechanical' and 'higher' reading skills, than average children taught in CES from the beginning.

2) The most noticeable superiority of 'phonics' children in Class I is in scores on tests of 'recognising' print in terms of sound, and in Class II in scores on 'Regulars' and 'Irregulars' only.

3) Practically all the 'mechanical' skills tested in this investigation are correlated highly, at one or other stage of learning to read, with both power and rate of comprehension.

4) A low correlation between 'mechanical' and 'higher' reading skills may indicate that the former skills, having once been sufficiently mastered, must be superseded. For instance, the correlation between comprehension and the 'translation' or 'Irregulars' was relatively low with all those groups of children who achieved high scores on tests involving 'translation'.

5) The results suggest that a phonemic notation (as represented by i.t.a.) helps to prepare a basis for the development of 'higher' reading skills in an average child. In Class I an average i.t.a. child scores highly on 'translation' but not on efficiency of 'reading proper'. At the same time, whatever the teaching medium used, a child in Class II with a high Reading Age usually shows a high efficiency in both power and rate of comprehension. But the i.t.a. group in Class II as a whole scores significantly higher on Reading

Age than the matched CES group, and it might be concluded that a fairly phonemic teaching medium is directly helpful in the early formation of some 'mechanical' skills which enable the average beginner to enlarge his reading vocabulary quite quickly, and that this vocabulary in turn promotes the child's efficiency in 'reading proper'.

6) The role of semi-ideography in the development of 'higher' reading skills is indicated by two sets of findings. First, although children who were taught to read by means of i.t.a. were not at that stage significantly superior to CES children in either rate or power of comprehension, yet once they had been transferred to CES, they became remarkably superior in both respects to children of the same age and I.Q. at school entry who had been taught to read by means of CES only. Secondly, adult readers scored significantly higher on comprehension tests when reading CES than in reading either IPA or P.Sh., even if they could write P.Sh. very much faster than the conventional orthography.

One of the main general conclusions to be drawn does seem to be that in average children a phonemic writing system is most conducive to the formation of elementary reading skills, while a semi-ideography promotes the development of 'higher' reading skills. The effects of a phonemic writing system are indicated by a comparison of the test results of children taught to read by different media (see Figure 11 on p. 127). All i.t.a. groups of children scored higher than the corresponding CES groups on certain 'mechanical' tests. In Class I, however, they did not score as highly on the two tests of rate of comprehension, and they were not superior to other groups in the tests of short-term memory for nonsense syllables and of power of comprehension. Thus it would seem that a phonemic writing system does not facilitate 'recognition' of print in the graphemic sense, nor does it *directly* assist comprehension.

The relatively low rate of comprehension would seem to indicate that these i.t.a. children analysed words into smaller units than did the other children. Their success in this analysis is evident from their very high scores on every test where 'translation' is involved more directly—'recognition' in the Graded Vocabulary Test, pronunciation of words found in texts, reading aloud of phrases on a moving tape, and 'translation' of unfamiliar spellings. At the same time this analysis seems to slow down the rate at which the younger i.t.a. children read: within the given time-limit for a comprehension test the total score does not differ from that of other children, but to complete as much as they can of the test paper—i.e. to reach the last sentence within their comprehension power—takes them a longer period of time. By contrast, after i.t.a. children have been transferred to CES, their rate of comprehension on both parts of the test becomes almost double that of children taught by CES throughout; their scores on power of comprehension also are higher than those of the Class II CES group, though the difference is less striking.

How can this apparent dichotomy in the results be explained? Of course, in view of the relatively small scale of this investigation, one cannot altogether rule out the possibility that certain children or schools participating in Experiment II enjoyed particularly favourable teaching facilities or other advantages that would mask or distort the influence of the media used. Nevertheless, it does seem possible to make some assessment of the relative influence of different writing systems, by comparing 'ratios of achievements' of various matched groups. These are shown by Figure 14. The abbreviations on the base-line stand for chronological age and for the twelve variables that were measured in any of the three experiments. The ordinates show the ratio between the achievements of the first and the second of the two groups mentioned in the key. Thus, if you follow the dotted line with the solid black triangles, you can read off on the vertical scale the ratios in which the 'Phonics' children of Class I surpassed (or, if the ratio is less than 1·0, fell below) the matched 'Look-Say' group. Then, if you compare this with the dotted line with the white triangles, you can see that for Class I children the teaching method seemed to make even more difference to their achievement than did the writing system—except in the easier of the tests on the perception of phrases, and (for obvious reasons) in the 'translation' of 'Irregulars'. By contrast, if you look at the continuous lines marked with white and black circles, you can see that for Class II children the results seem to have been affected less by the teaching method than by the writing system in which the children had first learnt to read. In three important respects—speed of finding words, 'translation' of 'Irregulars', and power of comprehension—the ratio for groups taught by different media is remarkably higher than the ratio for groups taught by different methods. Closely related to this are the very high i.t.a./CES ratios for rates of comprehension. Finally, the graph shows that, for adult readers, the CES/IPA and CES/P.Sh. ratios for rate of comprehension are relatively very high:

Figure 14: Ratios of group achievements in Classes I, II and III

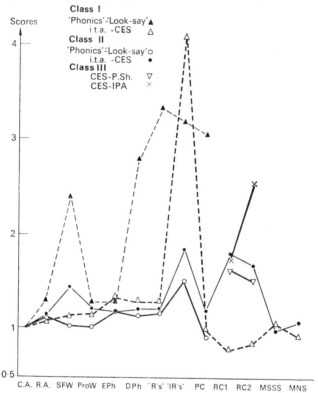

roughly, CES was understood at about twice the speed of either of the other systems. The difference between CES and P.Sh. decreased slightly as the sentences became more difficult; but the difference between rates of comprehension in reading CES and in reading a purely phonemic notation significantly increased with the difficulty of paragraphs.

All in all, then, it seems reasonable to conclude that the development of reading skills can be influenced at least as much by teaching media—in the sense of writing systems—as by teaching methods. This is of course borne out on a wider scale by the results so far reported in the i.t.a. project as a whole, of which the investigation here described is quite independent. Moreover, it seems possible to distinguish to some extent between the kinds of influence exerted by medium and method at different stages. Why is it that the average child taught to read with an emphasis on 'Phonics' has a lead in every respect in Class I, yet in Class II his achievement on the 'power of comprehension' test is relatively low (see Figure 10, p. 120)? Why is it that the average child who has been taught to read by means of i.t.a. has no significant lead in 'power of comprehension' over his CES counterpart in Class I (see Figure 11, p. 127), yet in Class II is significantly superior to him both in rate and power of comprehension?

This situation can perhaps be explained on the basis of the theoretical part of this study. At the early stages of learning to read, the average child has to rely on his experience of spoken language in order to 'translate' print into sound; but to do this 'translation' from CES requires a knowledge not only of the relationships between individual units, but also of the relationships between certain sequences of graphemes and certain phonemic chains. At the early stages, therefore, the acquisition of this skill to translate CES requires a good deal of oral drill. If this drill be given on a wide variety of texts, it will at first increase the child's vocabulary, which would account for a relatively high 'Power of Comprehension' at the earlier stages. But excessive drill of this sort would appear to be harmful in the long run, as it seems to develop the habit of an intensive inner speech to such an extent that a child will tend to use it even when he recognises the word by sight, and thus his efficiency in silent reading is impaired. Consequently, a few years later, the total amount of material that a predominantly 'Phonics-taught' child has read for himself may be less than that read by a child in the matched 'Look-Say' group who has subsequently been left more or less to his own method of coping with print.

The possible harmful effects of excessive oral drill seem to have been eliminated with the groups of children initially taught by means of i.t.a. The explanation is probably as follows. The average child taught to read by means of a fairly phonemic system learns not only to 'translate' the individual signs into the corresponding phonemes but also to blend these into spoken words relatively quickly and with less need for oral drill; the 'translation' into meaningful units requires less overt speech and less intervention from the teacher. Thus at the Class II stage he is using 'inner speech' to the best advantage, as is reflected in the high rate and power of his comprehension.

The importance of using different teaching media at different stages of learning to read is further brought out by studying the coefficients of correlation between scores on comprehension and on the 'mechanical' skills for various groups of children. As we noted previously, the degree of proficiency in 'mechanical' skills is generally not very relevant to the main goal of reading—the comprehension of printed messages. However, there are two groups—the older 'Look-Say' children in Experiment I, and the older CES children in Experiment II—for which these correlations are unusually high, which may indicate that for these children the comprehension of print is heavily dependent upon their ability to 'translate' print into sound. Finally, the majority of correlations referring to older i.t.a. children (Class II in Experiment II), though high, are still moderate in comparison with those of the corresponding group of CES children, whom the i.t.a. group surpassed in rate and power of comprehension. We might well interpret this as meaning that the i.t.a. children had developed the 'mechanical' reading skills suffic-iently—i.e. to the extent that their comprehension of print was not hindered by inability to 'translate' into phonemic terms where such 'translation' is called for—but that they had not over-developed these skills at the expense of the higher 'Gestalting' processes which make for efficiency in 'reading proper'.

"Normally, in psychology," writes P. E. Vernon, "it is impossible to prove a hypothesis, for though experiments may confirm certain predictions, there are always likely to be other implications which have not been explored." The investigations described in the two previous chapters are only a small part of all the study of reading that is now in progress, and many implications are still to be explored. The proposition that the use of a phonemic writing system for initial teaching promotes the development of some elementary reading skills is one that has been subjected to widespread public testing for almost a decade, and it is already possible to claim that such a system contributes also to the subsequent development of general reading ability in the average child. But we still do not know enough about *why* it has these effects—whether, for instance, a phonemic notation is indeed more conducive to the building up of reading vocabulary at an early age, or whether it simply gives the learner an essential confidence and more rapid rewards, or whether it has deeper and more lasting effects upon his perceptual processes. We need to know much more about *how* various teaching media influence the forma-tion of the visual 'field' in reading. To establish whether writing systems make any difference to the number of eye-fixations per line of print it would be necessary to use instruments that secure accurate observations and recording of eye movements. It is also desirable that further research be devoted to verifying the suggestion that a system such as CES has a positive influence in prompting the development of 'higher' reading skills. This is of considerable practical importance, because it would help in determining the right point of transfer from the initial teaching medium to conventional English spelling.

In that traditional orthography are encoded some of the great treasures of the world; the children who unknowingly contributed to this book have joined millions of others who have wandered in those "realms of gold". When they – or you – read Keats or space fiction or a newspaper or a book on education, an infinite number of patterns, some immediate, some more remote, are being interwoven concurrently to yield meanings. To interpret the written word is to gain access to information, to wisdom, to delight. In that complex activity there may be perceptual and psychological processes still 'higher' than those we have been able to examine in this book. We hope that what has been written on these pages may stimulate further research, and encourage those who are already engaged, at any level, in the investigation or teaching of reading.

Appendix A

An historical survey of some English spellings

As soon as we start to enquire into the discrepancies between the spelling and the pronunciation of present-day English, it becomes clear that there is no one simple explanation for them. To understand fully even a few dozen of the commonest instances would require an account of over a thousand years of European linguistic and cultural development. In our language is our history, and—it is sometimes maintained—our character. All that is attempted here is a rapid and elementary sketch, such as may serve to indicate the history of a few of the many words whose spelling causes difficulty or puzzlement or merely curiosity. The examples are chosen so as to include as many as possible of the words occurring in the test material described in Chapter 7. These word lists were of course drawn up originally with quite other considerations in mind, but they are purposely used again here as a means of suggesting the varied kinds of interest that a teacher or learner may find in both the forms and the meanings of almost any collection of English words. The full story of most of them, however, can be traced only by someone who gives himself the trouble and the pleasure of consulting the great *Oxford English Dictionary*.

Present-day conventional English spelling (referred to throughout this book as CES) can be described as 'mixed'—that is, neither completely phonetic nor completely ideographic—or at best as 'historically phonetic'. It has never been consistently phonemic. Some of the symbols it has used in the past have been phonemically redundant (as *c*, *q* and *x* are now) and others overburdened (like the notorious *gh*). The main reasons for the inconsistencies in CES are given in the following account, which proceeds more or less chronologically, though it must be remembered that many factors overlapped and interacted over long periods and, at least until the general spread of printed matter, varied in their effects from one region to another.

Nearly all the words in the English tongue that we say most often—like all but one of those that make up this sentence—come from the speech of our Anglo-Saxon forefathers who settled in these islands about fourteen hundred years ago. This language (usually known as Old English) was written down by the early Christian missionaries from Ireland, who used a Celtic variety of the Roman alphabet to record the words used by their converts. But Old English, being a Germanic language, contained some speech-sounds for which no equivalent symbol existed in Latin script. Therefore these early scribes supplemented the Latin alphabet in two ways.

The first was that they adopted two symbols from the heathen 'runic' writing, used by Germanic peoples for religious and magical inscriptions, and consisting mainly of straight lines such as could most easily be scratched on wood or stone. These two runic symbols usefully represented the sounds that were later written as 'w' and 'th'. But they passed out of general scribal use during the Middle English period (which may be roughly defined as between the Norman Conquest and the introduction of printing)—with one curious survival. The letter that had represented 'th' in old English looked something like a Y and long after its origin had been forgotten, Y continued to be used in a few very common words like *the* and *that*, in handwritten documents and in inscriptions, until the early eighteenth century. In an archaic sign like 'Ye olde shoppe', *Ye* represents only the pronunciation 'the'.

Secondly, the Old English alphabet included a new letter (ð), invented by putting a stroke through the Irish form of the Latin 'd'. This new letter also was used to represent a 'th' sound. There were in Old English, as in Modern English, two sounds that we represent by 'th': a voiced consonant as in *though, brother, bathe*, and an unvoiced consonant as in *think, thought, bath*. Thus, as the earliest English scribes had two letters available, it would have been possible for them to distinguish between these sounds; but in fact there seems to have been little consistency about the way the two symbols were used. Eventually, both letters were superseded by the 'th', under the influence of the French scribes writing after the Norman Conquest.

Conversely, some symbols in Old English were used to represent several different sounds. For instance, the letter ʒ corresponded to our *g* or *y*, representing the different initial consonants in the words ʒod (good) and ʒeonʒ (young), and in the second word had also to serve yet again, in combination with n, to represent the final consonant, which was sounded in Old English, as it still is in some Midland and Northern dialects.

Even at this early stage, then, we can trace two of the reasons why English spelling has never been consistently phonemic: there were more phonemes in the language than there were letters in the available alphabet, and the symbols that were available were haphazardly employed. Usually, each scribe solved his problems as best he could, without much reference to the practice of other writers in other places. Even if the idea of a conventionalised spelling had been conceivable then, the practical difficulties of applying it over a wide geographical area would have been almost insuperable.

The Old English words that form the basis of our language have a long history of continuous use, in the course of which many changes have taken place in both their pronunciation and their spelling. Among these words are most of our pronouns and possessive words (*I, you, he; mine, his*, etc.), conjunctions (*and, but, if*) and commonest adjectives and adverbs (*good, long, little, well*). Many of our most-needed verbs are Anglo-Saxon (*do, have, make, say, work*); others such as *bid* and *clip* have interesting histories of changes of meaning even if pronunciation and spelling have altered little. Our nouns for basic human relationships and activities are mostly of Old English derivation, though the words *father, mother* and *brother* have been made more alike in spelling than they originally were. *House* and *yard* are Old English too, as are *shelf* and *-wale* (as in *gunwale*), and the names of common animals, birds and trees, *horse, cow, crow, ousel, thrush, birch* and *oak*). We should notice here that the words now spelt *cow* and *house* (O.E. *cū, hūs*) had the same vowel sound—as they still do, though the sound itself has altered; but the word for *crow* (O.E. *crawe*) contained a different vowel, and *ousel* (O.E. *osle*) yet another. Changes of pronunciation later led to a variety of different ways of trying to represent these sounds in writing, with the confusing results that we now have. Especially complicated is the history of the pronunciation and spelling of English place names, many of which derive from words used either by the Anglo-Saxons or by the Norsemen who settled in the northern and eastern parts of England between the eighth and eleventh centuries. The elements *-caster, -chester* and *-cester* all derive from the Latin *castra* (the camp or garrison town of Roman times), and represent respectively the Latinate, Old English and French forms of that word.

Some puzzling features of CES can be traced back to origins in

Old English. CES is 'historically phonetic' in that some of its now silent letters represent sounds that were once pronounced. The modern *knight* is derived from O.E. *cniht*, in which every letter represented an actual speech-sound. These sounds were still to be heard when the word was being written down in the fourteenth century, so that Chaucer's spelling *knight* was still a phonetic one, and it has survived long after the *k* and *gh* have ceased to be sounded. The *w* in *sword* and the *g* in *gnaw* and *gnome* also represent what were once speech-sounds. In *wr*-words like *write* and *wrong*, the *w* was pronounced as late as the seventeenth century.

Within the limitations of the available script, English spelling began by being roughly phonetic. It became progressively less so, for two main reasons. One is the perennial and inescapable fact that no conventional system of spelling can ever keep pace with the changes in pronunciation that are always taking place in a living language. This was of course as true of the period between A.D. 700 and 1100 as of later times. Secondly, after the Norman Conquest, much of the writing of English was done by French scribes, who naturally made use of the spelling conventions of their own language, somewhat in the same way as English and French colonists of the eighteenth and nineteenth centuries did in trying to transliterate Oriental and African languages. Mostly they wrote down what they thought they heard, representing the native speech-sounds by the most nearly corresponding symbols that they knew. But at least the Normans and the English had similar alphabets and scripts, so that some of the Old English spelling habits could be retained.

For over two hundred years after the Norman Conquest, the language of the ruling classes in England—and therefore of nearly all official proceedings and records—was French, or rather, a progressively anglicised version of Norman French, which was different from 'Frenssh of Paris', as Chaucer knew even if his Prioress did not. But the vernacular did not die out; indeed, a continuous history can be traced for both its spoken and its literary forms. About the middle of the fourteenth century, with the emergence of London as a political and ecclesiastical centre, and of the East Midlands as the economic and cultural nucleus of the national life, the native dialect spoken in that area reasserted itself as the most important medium of communication and began to develop into the standard English of today. By the time of Chaucer (the end of the fourteenth century), the English language had undergone further changes of pronunciation as well as of grammar, and it had acquired a large admixture of French words. Of the words used in the test-material, the following all came into our language from French during the Middle English period, and even this small sample bears witness to the strong French influence upon the vocabulary of the law and the church and their administration, and the techniques both of war and of domestic and personal adornment:

agate, allege, attorney, cardinal, cavalry, certificate, chant, chart, cherish, conductor, confession, constable, docile, equity, impugn, pursuivant, signet, tablet, tress, triumphant, vine.

We may notice that most of these words have become so naturalised as to follow the usual phonetic and stress patterns of English. Some have kept features of the French spelling, but not the pronunciation (e.g. *impugn*); others—technical words like *attorney* and *pursuivant*—preserve something of the original pronunciation. Others again, like *signet,* have subsequently been changed in pronunciation because Renaissance scholars insisted that the word was derived from a Latin root (*signum*). *Vine* (Fr. *vigne*) has changed in pronunciation along with *wine* (O.E. *wīn*); but in the combination *vineyard,* the diphthongisation has not taken place, the shortening of the vowel perhaps being due to the stress on the first syllable. We may compare these mediaeval acquisitions from French with other words that entered English at a later stage, after the above-mentioned pronunciation changes had occurred: *pique* and *prestige* (originally meaning 'deception', 'imposture'), which came to us in the sixteenth and seventeenth century respectively, are still pronounced as in French. The word *gillyflower,* on the other hand, has been thoroughly naturalised: it is a corruption of the Old French *girofle,* with the last syllable assimilated to other *-flower* words, in the same way as the French *écrivisse* was made into the English *crayfish.* The word *mange* raises an interesting problem: there is some doubt whether it is derived from a corresponding Old French noun, or whether it is a 'back-formation' from *mangy* (Fr. *mangé*), i.e. that the *-y* has been regarded as it if were an English adjectival suffix, leading to the invention of the noun *mange.*

As was pointed out above, the French-trained scribes of the twelfth and thirteenth centuries had to write down many English words, and in doing so altered their spellings. Before the end of the Old English period, the sound represented by the letter *c* (originally always hard) had been modified in certain positions to the sound tʃ, and the difference was shown in Norman times by the use of the nearest French equivalent, *ch*, as in words like *child* (O.E. *cild*) and *birch* (O.E. *berc*). Thus the modern *chicken* corresponds to the O.E. *cicen* with very little change in the pronunciation. The use of the shortened form *chick* may have been influenced by the fact that *-en* was in Southern Middle English a fairly common plural ending (*oxen* and *brethren* survive). Conversely, the modern word *children* is due to the fact that an older and even rarer plural ending was *-er*, and when the form *childer* ceased to be readily recognisable as plural, the additional suffix *-en* was attached to it, by analogy with other plurals so formed.

Some other words of Old English origin that appear in our lists have curious histories in Middle English. Readers may like to look up *behalf* and *sheen*. *Aisle* is a complex product of at least two different words: one of them is the word *isle*, in which the *s* is at least etymologically correct because of the Latin *insula* from which the Old French word was derived. But the *s* was wrongly inserted also in the word *island* (from O.E. *igland*), and has never been pronounced in that word.

In the Middle English the symbol *gh* had to do hard service as the written equivalent of a variety of English consonant sounds; some of them are no longer pronounced (e.g. in *daughter, though, bough*); others survive in modified form (as in *laughter, tough*). At the same time the *ou* combination had to represent several different vowels. Moreover, some of the inconsistencies that survive in CES are in part the result of the fact that some pronunciations and spellings from dialects other than the East Midlands happened to be incorporated into what eventually became standard English.

The position was further complicated by the particularly rapid changes in pronunciation that took place in England during the fifteenth and sixteenth centuries. Between the death of Chaucer and the birth of Shakespeare, almost every vowel-sound in English had altered in quality; some that had hitherto been pure vowels became diphthongs, as was mentioned earlier. So complete and so relatively consistent was this process that it has been given the name of the Great Vowel Shift. It was followed, though more slowly, by changes in spelling habits. But before these changes could be generally adopted, the new invention of printing had begun to have the effect of standardising the written form of the language. The early printers in England, Caxton, de Worde and their successors, mostly followed the manuscripts they had in front of them, with the result that many Middle English conventions of spelling came to be preserved in print just at the time when they were ceasing to correspond to the spoken forms of the words. Spellings like *clerk* and *shew* once represented pronunciation much more closely than they do now. The sixteenth century, when the printed word was becoming most influential, and when spelling conventions were consequently beginning to be established, was a period of great changes, in both the vocabulary and the pronunciation of English, which were not reflected in the practice of the printers. The result is that wide discrepancies between the spoken word and its written counterpart have become as it were fossilised in print. Even so, considerable freedom in choice of spellings remained possible, and the First Folio edition (1623) of Shakespeare's plays is full of inconsistencies and revealing survivals. It was not until the eighteenth century that the idea of a standardised spelling was generally accepted.

The Renaissance revitalised the study of linguistic problems, and especially redirected attention to the classical languages. Not only were many new English words coined from Greek and Latin material, but also older acquisitions from these languages, which had come in by way of French, were re-examined and sometimes re-spelt. For instance, words that in the fourteenth century had been correctly spelt *dette, doute, receite,* as in French, began to be spelt *debt, doubt, receipt,* so as to show their connection with Latin originals, even though the *b* and *p* had never been sounded in English. (Alongside them we have *debit, dubiety* and *receptive* formed regularly direct from the Latin.) Similarly the *l* was introduced into *solder* (Fr. *soudure*), though it was not pronounced in all dialects.

Words derived from classical Greek, whether or not they have passed into English via Latin, tend to preserve the consonant sound of the original, e.g. *cachinnation, chasm, trochee,* as do more modern formations like *psychology,* though the initial *p* before *s* usually becomes silent, as it had done in older acquisitions like *psalm* (sometimes written *salm* in Old English). On the other hand, although *sceptic* retains the hard *c* as in the Greek *skeptikos* (perhaps to distinguish it from *septic*), the pronunciation of *sciatica* indicates its route via French, *cinema* has now ousted *kinema,* and *cyclamen* has been treated as analogous with *cycle* in respect of the consonants but not the vowels. Equally inconsistent has been our treatment of later borrowings from the classical languages. *Alibi* has been completely anglicised in all but spelling; *fulcrum* has been treated as analogous with *effulgent* rather than with *fulsome;* the invention *phaeton* (a somewhat pedantic eighteenth-century joke) preserves the first consonant sound of *Phaethon* but not the second (which indicates that it is of French coinage). Modern scientific language can be quite arbitrary in its use of classical words and forms: *fuchsia* is named after a German botanist, but ignores the German pronunciation; *schist* is from a Greek root, but has passed into English via French with the pronunciation of *sch-* influenced by the German.

The English, in their multifarious contacts with other peoples, have raided many languages. A few examples in our list are *cassia* (ultimately from Hebrew, via Greek and Latin); *cargo* and *cigar* from Spanish; and *sherbet*, from Persian, via Turkish. *Ballot*, a sixteenth-century acquisition from the Italian *ballotta* (a small ball used for voting), is now stressed according to the English pattern; *duet*, introduced two centuries later from the same language, is not. Etymologically, one of the most interesting words to appear on our list is *char*, regular as it is in spelling. It is really three words with different meanings and histories, though they look alike; that is, they are homonyms. One of them is Old English (a variant of *chore*); another is probably a back formation from *charcoal*; the third is an oriental (originally Chinese) word for 'tea'.

The differences between our modern spelling conventions and those used by Shakespeare, Milton, Bunyan, Dryden, and even Johnson, are in themselves a fascinating and rewarding topic of study; but we leave them to be explored by our readers with the help of other books. The relatively small changes in spelling that have taken place in the last two hundred and fifty years do not much help to explain the characteristic difficulties faced by anyone starting to learn or to teach CES.

The history of the English language provides the following reasons for the inconsistencies of our spelling: (i) the inadequacy of the available symbols—unless specially invented ones—to represent the whole range of phonemes in English at any time; (ii) haphazard application of available symbols; (iii) the effect of different scribal traditions; (iv) dialectical variations which may or may not be represented in a standard notation; (v) the influence of analogy, real or supposed; (vi) the influence of etymology, real or supposed; (vii) the fact that the treatment of words imported from other languages has varied according to the date of acquisition; (viii) the effect of the spread of the printed word in 'fixing' spelling; (ix) the fact that changes in pronunciation will be reflected in the standard written form of the language, if at all, only long after they have taken place. To these we may add the influence of literary tradition: the richer and more highly valued is the literature, the more resistance there will be to 'modernising' it, and the more archaic words and phrases from it will be embedded in the language.

Appendix B

Some more 'Irregulars' to be tested

The following is a list of English words which warrant consideration as being 'irregular' in the relationship between their spelling and the received pronunciation. They are offered simply as a sample of the material on which a teacher can base the prediction and analysis of error as suggested in Chapter 7. Not all of these words will be irregular for all grades of reader, as so much depends upon the reader's previous experience and upon the power of the analogies that he is able to draw. Some very common words, like *are* and *of*, which are uniquely irregular, soon cease to cause difficulty. At one stage, *climb* will clearly be irregular and *timber* will not; at a later stage, *climber* may appear to be no more evidently irregular than *bombastic*. At one stage the pronunciation of the *o* in *other* is irregular; but when a reader is familiar with *mother*, *brother* and *smother*, it is the word *bother* that seems irregular. Similarly, *earth* and *learn* eventually provide analogies for *dearth*, *earn* and *yearn*, but not for *hearth*. The grapheme-strings *chl-* and *chr-* become reliable to a degree that *ch* in other combinations does not. In each case the teacher must look carefully at the word and think of the possible pronunciations that it might suggest to the learner.

The list includes some words of foreign origin and pronunciation if they are in sufficiently common use to be encountered by a moderately advanced English learner. It is impossible to draw hard-and-fast distinctions. Words already cited in the test material are not included again. The selection is arranged as far as possible in the alphabetical order of the letters which appear to be most closely connected with the irregularity, first the consonant letters and then the vowel letters. Obviously there is a good deal of overlap, and some words are irregular in more than one respect, but no word is listed more than once. Occasionally the list includes a pair of related words of which either or both might be classified as irregular at different stages, e.g. *autumn, autumnal*. Variations of stress-pattern must be taken into account.

155

CONSONANTS

Letter b	orchestra	Letter f	forehead
bomb	archaic	of	shepherd
climb	architect	halfpenny	vehicle
dumb	archive		annihilate
succumb	anarchy	Letter g	exhaust
bombastic	chlorine	gaol	exhibit
doubt	chloroform	mortgage	exhilarate
debt	christian	gear	exhort
subtle	christen	geese	ghastly
subterfuge	chrome	geyser	ghost
	chronic	gig	ghoul
Letter c	chronicle	giggle	
concerto	avalanche	gilt	Letter j
violoncello	brochure	gill	bijou
special	douche	together	hallelujah
species	machine	begin	
blackguard	moustache	anger	Letter k
indict	nonchalance	bogey	knave
victuals	parachute	lager	knee
yacht	chagrin	finger	knight
schedule	chalet	forget	knock
schism	chamois	forgive	know
scholar	champagne	hunger	knuckle
school	chaperon	hanger	
schooner	charade	linger	Letter l
scheme	chassis	barrage	alms
schizophrenic	chauffeur	camouflage	calf
sandwich	chef	garage	calm
epoch	chic	massage	chalk
stomach	chicanery	sabotage	could
ache	chivalrous	beige	half
chaos	chute	rouge	folk
character		bourgeois	malmsey
choleric	Letter d	lingerie	salmon
chorus	grandson	regime	colonel
chord	handsome		
chorister	handkerchief	Letter h	Letter n
anchor	landscape	heir	autumn
echo	grandeur	honest	autumnal
mechanic	soldier	honour	column

condemn	mosquito	husband	mistletoe
damn		muslin	boatswain
hymn	*Letter r*	wisdom	waistcoat
solemn	iron	dessert	whistle
		dissolve	
Letter p	*Letter s*	possess	*Letter w*
pneumatic	basin	scissors	who
psalm	crusade	rescind	whole
cupboard	episode	scythe	whoop
raspberry	mason		wrap
receipt	nuisance	*Letter t*	wreck
Stephen	sausage	thyme	write
nephew	philosophy	though	wrath
	prosecute	apathy	wreath
Letter q	disable	atheist	wrong
quay	research	author	sword
queue	resource	cathedral	two
conquer	misled	ether	answer
exchequer	absolve	ethic	gunwale
etiquette	clumsy	lithograph	
lacquer	crimson	method	*Letter x*
liqueur	observe	pathos	xerograph
liquor	whimsical	chestnut	xylophone
mannequin	gosling	Christmas	

VOWELS

Letter a	alum	banal	portrait
acre	attaché	barrage	reconnaissance
amiable	cavil	cantata	gauge
bass	enamel	lava	draught
emaciated	fathom	promenade	chauffeur
patriarch	malice	soprano	mauve
almond	gravel	saga	restaurant
almoner	madrigal	mirage	scarce
are	palate	chaos	
lager	plateau	haemorrhage	*Letter e*
palaver	sacrament	maelstrom	abbreviate
appal	sacrosanct	plaid	alleviate
palsy	stature	plait	amenity
amoral	ravel	archaic	appreciate
catastrophe	valiant	plantain	decent

edict	jealous	libellous	polish
precept	leaden	lichen	posture
pretext	pheasant	align	profligate
scenic	realm	malign	prodigal
strategic	treacherous	meringue	provost
vehement	zealot	alibi	plover
inclement	break	cyclical	slovenly
level	steak	guinea	onion
leper	European	insidious	one
metal	beatitude	privy	only
metric	meander	signal	compass
pedant	reality	sinew	money
preface	create	triple	mongrel
prelude	breeches	vitrous	effrontery
sever	eider	vitriol	covenant
severe	geyser	virile	covet
venom	kaleidoscope	vigour	shovel
refuge	sleight	capricious	worship
suede	seismograph	caprice	worth
clerk	deign	chemise	borough
dearth	feign	clique	worsted
hearse	freight	litre	worst
pearl	inveigh	fatigue	catalogue
yearn	heinous	intrigue	dialogue
eyrie	veil	marine	obese
hearth	heifer	sardine	posterior
hearken	leisure	technique	blood
acme	deity	unique	flood
anemone	albeit	propriety	brooch
epitome	forfeit		zoological
finale	sovereign	*Letter o*	poem
creosote	sew	betrothed	canoe
theory	bureau	comatose	manoeuvre
geography	plateau	comb	coincide
leopard	beauty	tomb	connoisseur
jeopardy	bureaucracy	gross	cousin
deodorant	bureaucratic	nomenclature	tough
breakfast		ochre	dough
cleanse	*Letter i*	abolish	shoulder
dealt	ivory	bother	bouquet
endeavour	hibernate	grovel	route

uncouth	push	guard	extinguish
you	puss	guarantee	sanguine
youth	luscious	assuage	build
young	study	persuade	guilt
flourish	truculent	suave	guitar
furlough	burgh	language	biscuit
	furry	duet	circuit
Letter u	bury	guess	fruit
rhubarb	qualify	guest	suit
cuckoo	quantity	catalogue	suite
buffet	quarrel	harangue	buy
pulpit	quaff	tongue	buoy

Appendix C

A list of homophones

Homophones . . . form indeed one of the features of the English vocabulary which have to be taken seriously into account before it can be decided whether the present orthography, with a standing of some three centuries, can be usefully modified or replaced by one on a more phonetic basis.
(W. A. CRAIGIE, Some Anomalies of Spelling, S.P.E. Tracts, 1942, No. 59, p. 331.)

The following list is not exhaustive; nor probably can it be made so, since pronunciations vary from place to place and from time to time. Included here are some sets that are near-homophones in certain regional or social dialects, though distinguishable in others. It is *not* suggested that these spellings should be directly taught in pairs. A sounder approach will usually be to associate each of the words separately, when occasion arises, with familiar analogues, e.g. *alms* with *almond* and *calm*, *bier* with *pier* and *tier*, etc. The important thing is that the teacher should anticipate the possibilities of confusion, and devise systematic ways of overcoming them.

a	:	eh		bad	:	bade	
ail	:	ale		bail	:	bale	
aisle	:	isle	: I'll	ball	:	bawl	
all	:	awl		bare	:	bear	
alms	:	arms		baron	:	barren	
aloud	:	allowed		beach	:	beech	
air	:	heir	: ere	beer	:	bier	
are	:	r		bell	:	belle	
area	:	airier		berg	:	burg	
aren't	:	aunt		berry	:	bury	
ascent	:	assent		berth	:	birth	
ate	:	eight	: eyot	blew	:	blue	
				boar	:	bore	
b	:	be	: bee	board	:	bored	: bawd

bole	: boll	: bowl		descent	: dissent		
bow	: beau			dew	: due		
bow	: bough			die	: dye		
boy	: buoy			doe	: dough		
born	: borne			dost	: dust		
brake	: break			draft	: draught		
bread	: bred			doer	: dour		
breach	: breech			done	: dun		
but	: butt						
buy	: by	: bye		ease	: e's		
buyer	: byre			ewe	: you	: yew	: u
				ewes	: use	: u's	: yews
c	: sea	: see		eyed	: I'd		
calk	: cork	: caulk					
call	: caul			faint	: feint		
calves	: carves			fair	: fare		
caught	: court			fate	: fete		
cause	: caws			faun	: fawn		
caw	: core	: corps		feat	: feet		
cent	: scent	: sent		file	: phial		
ceiling	: sealing			fill	: Phil		
cell	: sell			fir	: fur		
cellar	: seller			flea	: flee		
cereal	: serial			flew	: flue	: flu	
chased	: chaste			floe	: flow		
cheap	: cheep			flour	: flower		
check	: cheque			for	: fore	: four	
choler	: collar			formally	: formerly		
chute	: shoot			fort	: fought		
cite	: sight	: site					
climb	: clime			g	: gee		
coarse	: corse	: course		gait	: gate		
colonel	: kernel			gamble	: gambol		
council	: counsel			gees	: g's		
crews	: cruise			gilt	: guilt		
current	: currant			gnatty	: natty		
				gnaw	: nor		
d	: de	: dee		grate	: great		
dam	: damn			grater	: greater		
daw	: door			groan	: grown		
dear	: deer			guessed	: guest		

hail	:	hale		
hair	:	hare		
hall	:	haul		
hay	:	hey		
heal	:	heel		
hear	:	here		
heard	:	herd		
hew	:	hue		
high	:	hie		
higher	:	hire		
him	:	hymn		
hoard	:	horde		
hoarse	:	horse		
hoes	:	hose		
hole	:	whole		
holy	:	wholly		
hour	:	our		
humorous	:	humerus		
hock	:	hough		

I	:	aye	:	eye
idle	:	idol		

j	:	jay
jam	:	jamb

k	:	kay		
key	:	quay		
knap	:	nap		
knead	:	need		
knew	:	new		
knight	:	night		
knit	:	nit		
knot	:	not		
know	:	no		
knows	:	nose	:	no's

lair	:	layer		
lane	:	lain		
laps	:	Lapps	:	lapse
law	:	lore		

lea	:	lee		
lead	:	led		
lessen	:	lesson		
liar	:	lier	:	lyre
lie	:	lye		
lightening	:	lightning		
loan	:	lone		
loot	:	lute		
low	:	lo		

made	:	maid		
mail	:	male		
main	:	mane		
maize	:	maze		
mare	:	mayor		
matrices	:	mattresses		
mead	:	meed		
meat	:	meet	:	mete
medal	:	meddle		
might	:	mite		
missed	:	mist		
moat	:	mote		
moor	:	more		
morning	:	mourning		

naval	:	navel	
nay	:	neigh	
none	:	nun	

o	:	oh
oar	:	ore
one	:	won
our	:	hour

p	:	pea				
pail	:	pale				
pain	:	pane				
pair	:	pear	:	pare		
pause	:	paws	:	pores	:	pours
peace	:	piece				

peak : peke : pique
peal : peel
peer : pier
peninsula : peninsular
place : plaice
plain : plane
plait : plat
plum : plumb
pole : Pole : poll
poor : pore : pour
practice : practise
pray : prey
principal : principle
profit : prophet

q : cue : queue

rain : rein : reign
raise : rays
reach : retch
read : red
real : reel
rest : wrest
right : rite : write
ring : wring
road : rode : rowed
roe : row
rose : rows
role : roll
rote : wrote
rough : ruff
route : root
rye : wry

sail : sale
sane : seine
sauce : source
saw : sore : soar
sawed : soared : sword
scene : seen
sea : see

seam : seem
seas : sees : seize
sew : so : sow
shear : sheer
shore : sure
sighs : size
sleight : slight
sloe : slow
sole : soul
son : sun
sort : sought
stake : steak
stare : stair
steal : steel
steps : steppes
stile : style
stationary : stationery
stork : stalk
suite : sweet

t : tea : tee
tail : tale
talk : torque
tare : tear
taught : taut
tears : tiers
teas : tease
their : there
threw : through
throe : throw
throne : thrown
tied : tide
time : thyme
to : too : two
told : tolled

vain : vein : vane
vale : veil

waist : waste
wait : weight

ware	:	wear	:	where	
way	:	weigh	:	whey	
we	:	wee			
weak	:	week			
weal	:	wheel			
which	:	witch			

whin	:	win
whither	:	wither
wood	:	would
y	:	why
yoke	:	yolk

Bibliography

General, including Chapter 1 and Appendix A

BAUGH, A. C. *History of the English Language*, Routledge, 1951

BOLTON, W. F. *A Short History of Literary English*, London, E. Arnold, 1967

DOWNING, J. A. (1) *The i.t.a. Reading Experiment*, London University Press, 1964; (2) *The i.t.a. Symposium*, London University Press, 1967

FRY, D. B. "Experimental Evidence for the Phoneme", in D. B. Fry (ed.) *In Honour of Daniel Jones*, London University Press, 1964

GIMSON, A. C. (1) *An Introduction to the Pronunciation of English*, London, E. Arnold, 1962; (2) "Phonetic Change and the R P Vowel System", in D. B. Fry (ed.) above

KAINZ, FRIEDRICH. *Psychologie der Sprache*, Stuttgart, Enke, 1956

PETERS, MARGARET L. *Spelling: Caught or Taught?*, London, Routledge and Kegan Paul, 1967

POTTER, SIMEON. *Our Language*, London, Penguin, 1957

QUIRK, RANDOLPH. *The Use of English* (2nd edn.), with supplements by A. C. Gimson and J. Warburg, London, Longman, 1968

SCHONELL, F. J. *Reading and Spelling Tests*, London, Oliver and Boyd, 1955

TUCKER, SUSIE I. *English Examined*, Cambridge, Univ. Press, 1961

VALLINS, G. H. (revised by D. G. Spragg). *Spelling*, London, Deutsch, 1965

WATTS, A. F. *The Language and Mental Development of Children*, London, Harrap, 1944

WRENN, C. L. *The English Language*, London, Methuen, 1949

Chapter 2: (i) Attempts at spelling reform

ARCHER, WILLIAM. "The Esthetic Argument", *SSS Pamphlet*, No. 4, 1909

DOWNING, J.A. "The Relationship between Reading Attainment and the Inconsistency of English Spelling at the Infants School Stage", *Br. J. of Ed. Psychol.*, Vol. 32, 1962

ELLIS, A. J. (1) *A Plea for Phonetic Spelling*, London, 1848; (2) "On Glosik", *Tracts Philol. Soc.*, 1870/2

HANSARD. Act 54, 1949: "Spelling Reform Bill"

RIPPMAN, WILLIAM. "Professor Lounsbury on English Spelling Reform", *SSS Pamphlet*, No. 7, 1911

SKEAT, W. W. *An Etymological Dictionary of the English Language*, pp. 762–771, 1882

WIJK, AXEL. *Regularised English*, Almquist & Wiksell, 1959

(*ii*) *Methods and rules*

CATTELL, JAMES MCKEEN. "Über die Zeit der Erkennung von Schriftzeichen, Bildern u. Farben", *Philosophische Studien*, No. 2, pp. 635–650

CRAIGIE, SIR WILLIAM. (1) *The Pronunciation of English*, London, 1917; (2) *English Spelling—Its Rules and Reasons*, New York, 1927

DEWEY, JOHN. "The Primary-Education Fetich", *Forum*, 1898

DIACK, HUNTER. *Reading and the Psychology of Perception*, Nottingham, 1960

ELLIS, A. J. "Spelling Difficulty and Its Remedy", *Tracts Philol. Soc.*, 1870/2

HART, JOHN (Chester Heralt). (1) *An Orthographie*, London, 1569; (2) *A Methode . . . to Read English*, London, 1570

NARES, ROBERT. *Elements of Orthoepy*, London, 1784

SCHONELL, F. J. *The Psychology and Teaching of Reading*, London, 1961

SHERIDAN, THOMAS. (1) *A Discourse*, Cambridge, 1759; (2) *Course of Lectures in Elocution*, 1762; (3) *Lectures on the Art of Reading*, 1775

WALLIS, JOHN. "A letter to Robert Boyle", *Philosophical Tracts*, 1670

(*iii*) *Modern investigators*

BURT, SIR CYRIL. *A Psychological Study of Typography*, Cambridge, 1959

LEE, W. R. *Spelling Irregularity and Reading Difficulty in English*, NFER 1960

LEWIS, M. M. *The Importance of Illiteracy*, London, 1953

LUCKIESH, M. L. and MOSS, F. K. *Reading as a Visual Task*, London, 1942

POULTON, E. C. "Effects of Printing Types and Formats on the Comprehension of Scientific Journals", *Nature*, 1959

TINKER, M. A. "Effects of Angular Alignment . . .", *Br. J. Ed. Psychol.*, 1956

VERNON, P. E. *Personality Assessment*, London, 1964

Chapter 3

BARTLETT, SIR FREDERIC. *Thinking*, Allen & Unwin, 1958

BOULDING, K. E. *The Image*, University of Michigan Press, 1961

BRADLEY, HENRY. *Spoken and Written English*, Oxford, 1919

CHOMSKY, NOAM: See via Lyons, John, below

COURTENAY, JEAN B. DE. Versuch einer Theorie Phonetischer Alternationen, Strassburg, 1895

CRAIGIE: See under *Chapter 2*: (ii)

CRYSTAL, DAVID, *What is Linguistics?*, London, E. Arnold, 1968

DOLLARD, J. and MILLER, N. E. *Personality and Psychotherapy*, New York, 1950

ELLSON, D. G. "Hallucinations Produced by Sensory Conditioning", *J. Experim. Psychol.*, 1941

HULL, C. L. *Principles of Behaviour*, London, Appleton, 1943

LYONS, JOHN. (1) *Introduction to Theoretical Linguistics*, Cambridge at University Press, 1968; (2) *Chomsky*, London, Fontana, 1970

MADSEN, K. B. *Theories of Motivation*, Copenhagen, 1959

MILLER, N. E. and DOLLARD, J. *Social Learning and Imitation*, London, Kegan Paul & Co., 1945

MURRAY, GILBERT. "Some Opinions", *SSS Pamphlet*, No. 5, 1926

OSGOOD, C. E. *Methods and Theory in Experimental Psychology*, New York, O.U.P., 1953

SAPIR, EDWARD. "Sound Patterns in Language", *Language*, No. 1, 1925

VERNON, M. D. *Backwardness in Reading*, Cambridge University Press, 1958

WALTER, W. G. *The Living Brain*, London, Duckworth, 1953

Chapter 4

BUSWELL, G. T. (1) *A Laboratory Study of the Reading in Modern Foreign Languages*, New York, Macmillan, 1928; (2) *How Adults Read*, University of Chicago, 1937

CATTELL, JAMES MCKEEN: See *Chapter 2*: (ii)

DODGE, RAYMOND. "An Experimental Study of Visual Fixation", *Psychol. Monogr.*, 8, No. 4, 1907

JAVAL, EMILE. *Physiologie de la Lecture et de L'Écriture*, Paris, Felix Alcan, 1906

POULTON, E. C. (1) "A Note on Printing to Make Comprehension

Easier", *Ergonomics*, No. 3, 1960; (2) "Peripheral Vision, Refractoriness and Eye Movements in Fast Oral Reading", *Br. J. Psychol.*, 1962

VERNON, M. D. (1) "The Movements of the Eyes in Reading", *Med. Res. Council:* Special Report Series, No. 148, 1930; (2) *The Experimental Study in Reading*, Cambridge University Press, 1931

Chapter 5

BALLARD, P. B. *Mental Tests*, London, Hodder & Stoughton, 1920

BLOOMFIELD, LEONARD and BARNHART, C. L. *Let's Read*, Detroit, Wayne State University Press, 1961

BUSWELL, G. T. *Non-Oral Reading*, University of Chicago Press, 1945

COURTENAY, JEAN B. DE: See *Chapter 3* above and in Jakobson, 1964, below

EDFELDT, ÅKE W. *Silent Speech and Silent Reading*, University of Stockholm, 1959

FLESH, RUDOLF. *Why Johnny Can't Read*, New York, Harper, 1955

GILBERT, DOROTHY WILCOX. *Breaking Reading Barrier*, Prentice-Hall, New York, 1959

JAGGER, J. H. *The Sentence Method of Teaching Reading*, Nelson, London, 1929

JAKOBSON, ROMAN. (1) *Technical Preliminaries to Speech Analysis*, Mass. Inst. Technol., University of Mass., 1955; (2) "Linguistic Typology of Aphasic Impairments", In A. V. C. Reuck (ed.) *Disorders of Language*, London, J. A. Churchill, 1964

JONES, DANIEL. (1) "Concrete and Abstract Sounds", *Third International Congress of Phonet. Soc.*, Phon. Lab. Univ. Ghent, 1938; (2) *The Phoneme—Its Nature and Use*, Cambridge, Heffer, 1949; (3) *The History and Meaning of the Term 'Phoneme'*, London, University College, 1964

LEWIS, M. M. and GULLIFORD, R. 'Language and Environment', B.B.C. publ. of *Ideas in Education*, 1965

LEWIS, M. M. *Language, Thought and Personality in Infancy and Childhood*, London, Harrap, 1963

YOUNG, W. E. "The Relation of Reading Comprehension and Retention to Hearing Comprehension and Retention", *J. Experim. Ed.*, No. 5, 1936

ZHUROVA, L. E. "The Development of Analysis of Words into their Sounds by Pre-school Children", *Soviet Psychology and Psychiatry*, Vol. II, London, 1963

Chapter 6

BUSWELL, G. T. "The Relationship between Perceptual and Intellectual Processing in Reading", California, *J. Ed. Res.*, No. 8, 1957

CRAIGIE, W. A. Problems of Spelling Reform, *S.P.E. Tract* 63, 1944

EHRENFELS, C. VON. "On Gestalt-Qualities", *Psychol. Rev.*, 44, 1937

ELKONIN, D. B. "The Psychology of Mastering the Elements of Reading", in J. & B. Simon (ed.), *Educational Psychology in U.S.S.R.*

GUBA, EGON. "Eye-Movements in TV Viewing", *Communication Review*, No. 12, 1964

HEBB, D. O. *The Organization of Behaviour*, New York, Wiley, 1949

HUNT, J. MCV. "Experience and the Development of Motivation", *Child Development*, No. 31, 1960

KIRK, S. A. "How Johnny Learns to Read", *Exceptional Children*, No. 22, 1956

KOFFKA, KURT. *Principles of Gestalt Psychology*, London, 1950

LASHLEY, K. S. "The Problem of Serial Order in Behaviour", in Sol Saporta (ed.) *Psycholinguistics*, New York, 1961

MACINTYRE, A. C. *The Unconscious*, London, Routledge, 1958

MADSEN, K. B.: See *Chapter 3* above

OSGOOD, C. E. "On Understanding and Creating Sentences", *Amer. Psychologist*, No. 18, 1963

PASSY, PAUL. *La Phonétique et ses Applications*, I.P.A. ed., 1929

PIAGET, JEAN. *Les Mechanismes Perceptifs*, Presses Univ. de France, 1961

PILLSBURY, W. B. and MEADER, C. L. *The Psychology of Language*, New York, Appleton & Co., 1928

TERMAN, SIBYL. *Reading—Chaos and Cure*, New York, McGraw-Hill, 1958

WHATMOUGH, JOSHUA. *Language*, London, Secker & Warburg, 1956

Chapter 7

DEWEY, GODFREY. *Relative Frequency of English Speech Sounds*, Harvard University Press, 1923

JAKOBSON, ROMAN. See *Chapter 5*, (1), above

PRATT, FLETCHER. *Secret and Urgent*, London, 1939

VERNON, M. D. "The Perceptual Processes in Reading", *The Reading Teacher*, No. 13, 1959

WALTER, W. G. "Features in the Electro-physiology of Mental Mechanisms", in D. Richter (ed.) *Perspectives in Neuropsychiatry*, London, H. K. Lewis, 1950